6th BIBLE READING MARATHON
A 27-Week Topical Bible Reading Schedule

Images of the

Master

From the Apostle John
...eyewitnesses of His majesty

The Bible Reading Marathon is designed to encourage regular reading of the Bible.

We believe the Bible is the inerrant, inspired Word of God.

We believe regular reading of the Bible builds faith in God.

We believe that the Christian's life is faith in action.

We believe regularly reading the Bible is a habit for a faithful Christian.

ACKNOWLEDGEMENTS

Copy Reviewed by
Kevin Boyd
Debbie Paine
Marie Weeks

Growing Panes Articles by
G. R. Holton

Cover Photo by
John Klimko

SCRIPTURE TEXTS CONTRIBUTORS

Homer Anderson
Myra Anderson
Kevin Boyd
Byron Brown
Janet Brown
Cheryle & Donny Bryan
Francine Coppage
Jerry Deloach
Richard Hamlen
Ruth Harrison
Kenny Holton
G. R. Holton
John Hunt
John & Marilyn King
John Klimko
B. J. & Don Lockey
Carol McLeod
Mike Paine
Debbie Paine
Carrie Seat
Don Seat
Toni Webb
Marie Weeks
Leon Weeks
Ronnie West
Michael Willis

SPONSORED AND DEVELOPED BY THE CENTRAL AVENUE CHURCH OF CHRIST
304 EAST CENTRAL AVENUE - VALDOSTA, GEORGIA
PHONE: (229) 242-6115 <central@cacoc.com>
Website: www.cacoc.com

6th BIBLE READING MARATHON

Images of the MASTER

From the Apostle John

A 27-WEEK TOPICAL BIBLE READING SCHEDULE

General Editor: **G. R. Holton**

Copy Reviewers: **Kevin Boyd * Debbie Paine * Marie Weeks**

Cover Photo: **John Klimko**

Growing Panes Articles: **G. R. Holton**

Published by

GROWING PANES, INC.

3543 Raintree Drive

Valdosta, Georgia 31601

Contact: grholton@yahoo.com

ISBN: 978-0-9905499-6-3

ISBN: 9 780990 549963

Printed by CreateSpace, An Amazon.com Company

Available from Amazon.com, CreateSpace.com, Growing Panes, Inc.,

and other retail outlets

Images of the Master

From the Writings of the Apostle John

Page:		Topic for the Week:	Basic Scripture:	Scriptures Contributors:
4		Make it a Habit!		
5		Bible Study Will Improve your Prayer Life		Kerry Holton
6		Make the Commitment		
7		The Power of Love		Author Unknown
8	Week 1:	When God Became a Man	John 1:1 – 2:12	G. R. Holton
	Week 2:	Building Belief in God's Son	John 2:13 – 4:26	Homer Anderson
	Week 3:	Many Believed in Jesus	John 4:27- 4:54	Myra Anderson
11	Growing Pane Milepost 3	The Word Became Flesh		
	Week 4:	Opposition to Belief in Jesus	John 5:1-47	Carol McLeod
	Week 5:	Opposition and Discipleship	John 6:1-71	Kevin Boyd
	Week 6:	Growing Opposition to Christ	John 7:1-53	Michael Willis
	Week 7:	Believers and Opposition	John 8:1 – John 9:41	Janet Brown
16	Growing Pane Milepost 7	God's Watchful Eye		
	Week 8:	Good Shepherd or A Demon	John 10:1 – John 11:57	Cheryle & Donny Bryan
	Week 9:	Jesus: King of Kings	John 12:1 – 50	Francine Coppage
	Week 10:	Son of Man to Son of God	John 13:1 – John 14:21	Jerry Deloach
	Week 11:	Relationships of Believers	John 15:1 – John 16:15	Richard Hamlen
21	Growing Pane Milepost 11	God was Not Finished with Me Yet		
	Week 12:	Jesus Prays for Believers	John 16:16–John 17:26	Ruth Harrison
	Week 13:	Arrest and Trials of Jesus	John 18:1-40	Kenny Holton
	Week 14:	His Death and Resurrection	John 19:1-John 20:10	John Hunt
	Week 15:	Appearances of Jesus	John 20:11-John 21:14	Marilyn & John King
26	Growing Pane Milepost 15	My Life in God's Hands		
	Week 16:	Fellowship with God	John 21:15-1 John 2:27	John Klimko
	Week 17:	Conditions of Fellowship	1 John 2:28-1 John 5:3	Betty Joyce & Don Lockey
	Week 18:	Love: Keep His Commandments	1 John 5:4-Revelation 1:20	Mike Paine
	Week 19:	Images of the Master's Bride	Revelation 2:1-29	Debbie Paine
31	Growing Pane Milepost 19	The Future Direction of My Life		
	Week 20:	Churches and The Master	Revelation 3:1 – 4:11	Carrie Seat
	Week 21:	Worthy is the Lamb of God	Revelation 5:1- 8:5	Don Seat
	Week 22:	Tribulations and Trials	Revelation 8:6 – 11:19	Toni Webb
	Week 23:	The Woman and The Beasts	Revelation 12:1– 13:18	Leon Weeks
	Week 24:	Judgment on the Earth	Revelation 14:1-18:19	Marie Weeks
	Week 25:	Heaven Rejoices	Revelation 18:20-19:21	Ronnie West
	Week 26:	The Final Victory	Revelation 20:1-21:8	Byron Brown
39	Growing Pane Milepost 26	Nothing to Be Afraid of...		
	Week 27:	BONUS: A Victory Lap	Revelation 21:9-22:21	G. R. Holton
41	Race Review Quiz			
	Back Cover		The Pulpit	

Make it A Habit!

Habits are usually instilled over time by responses we make in our lives. Effective parenting not only produces our family traditions, but also the behaviors we do by rote...like brushing our teeth, or taking a bath. Many social habits are instilled early, like learning to be courteous by saying "Thank you" and "Please." We all know the lifetime values in developing good study habits. Usually they result in good grades in school and steady promotions in life.

It's A Matter of Choice...and Training!

Good habits come from good practices. God's Word says it like this, *"Train up a child in the way he should go, And when he is old he will not depart from it (Proverb 22:6).* Each day is a "training day" for disciples of Christ. Each day we are instilling behaviors that will become rote habits. The repetitions and rote way we do the same thing on a regular basis is what produces habits. If we do good things *regularly* we will develop *good habits!* Proverb 4:23 says, *"Keep your heart with all diligence, For out of it spring the issues of life."*

Let me suggest a number of GOOD HABITS to do regularly:

- The habit of praying to God (Our Father).
- The habit of going to church (God's family).
- The habit of giving to the Lord (Our Savior).
- The habit of reading your Bible (God's Word).

The *Bible Reading Marathon* is based on *Charles Duhigg's three-part *"habit formation"* formula:

A. *The Cue,* or trigger, that begins the habit-forming cycle. The Marathon schedule includes posted scriptures, a time-table for reading, and beginning and ending cues.

B. *The Routine,* or the behavior patterns, that must become repetitive over time. On a regular (or daily) basis, you will repeat the same behavior, i. e., complete the Bible reading schedule.

C. *The Rewards,* or the positive, good feeling you experience for completing the behavior and completing the course. In addition, runners in the Bible Reading Marathon enjoy the knowledge of being blessed by pleasing God.

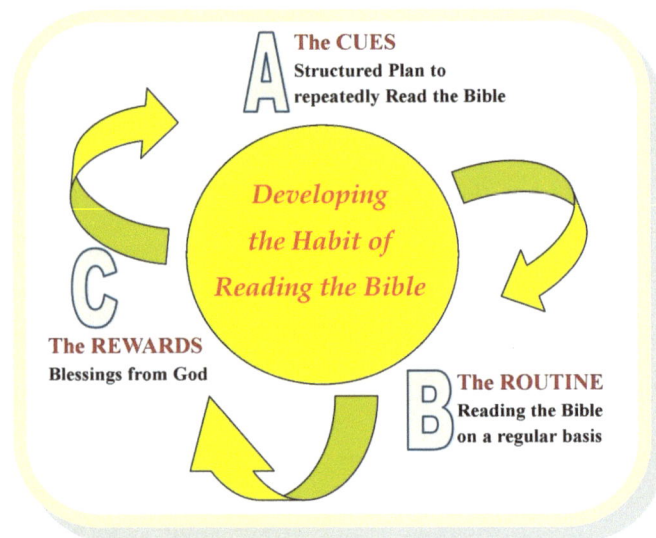

The CUES
Structured Plan to repeatedly Read the Bible

Developing the Habit of Reading the Bible

The REWARDS
Blessings from God

The ROUTINE
Reading the Bible on a regular basis

This same cycle can produce *bad habits.* Imagine how the habits resulting in addictions (such as drug or sexual addictions) develop. A person "looks upon" (the Cue) a woman to "lust after her" (the Routine) and gives in to the "temptation" (the Rewards) to become sexually immoral. Over time a bad habit is formed (chained-bad-behaviors-practiced) that destroys lives.

The Bible Reading Marathon is *a tool* to help you develop the *good* habit of regularly reading your Bible! Strong "good" habits are hard to break. Regular Bible reading is a good habit. Use the next twenty-seven weeks to form the habit of regular Bible reading! The rewards are awesome! Read Psalm 119. God's word is truly *"A lamp unto our feet and a light unto our pathways."*

The Power of Habit, Random House, New York, NY 2012

Daily Bible Study
Will Improve Your Prayer Life!

By Kerry Holton, Ph.D.

One of the things I've learned from the prophet Jeremiah in our daily study of his writings is how to improve my prayer life. For me, Jeremiah has modeled how to talk to God.

How so? Let me explain. The book of Jeremiah is unique among the prophetic books because of a remarkable group of utterances which are usually referred to as the "confessions" of Jeremiah. Some of these confessions are actually dialogues in which God responds to Jeremiah's remarks. Others are not. Each of them provides a rich study into the kind of prayer life with God that he finds acceptable. Let me give you some examples.

"Lord, I'm Taking You to Court!"

In Jeremiah 11 we learn that the people of Anathoth, Jeremiah's hometown, were conspiring to kill him. None too happy about it, the prophet takes God to court. Now, he prefaces his complaint with the trusting and respectful: *"You will be right, O Lord, when I lay charges against you,"* but then he lets it fly. He wants to know why the guilty prosper, that the treacherous thrive, while those who seek after God are like sheep led to the slaughter (Jeremiah 12:1-5).
God listens to Jeremiah's complaint, then gives it right back to him: *"If running a footrace has worn you out, how do you hope to vie with horses?"* (12:5). It's as if God is saying, "Get off your pity-pot, Jeremiah. No one said that serving as my prophet would be easy."

"Lord, I Feel that You've Abandoned Me!"

In chapter 15, Jeremiah cries out to God that he has been faithful in the discharge of his task despite the loneliness and hatred that were his lot. He expresses the fact that he had accepted God's calling, but that he felt he had been abandoned. And whom does he blame? You guessed it; he blames God. *"Under the weight of your hand I sat alone,"* Jeremiah brazenly declares. Then, he says: *"Truly, you are to me like a deceitful brook, like waters that fail"* (15:17,18). He is comparing God to a stream that goes dry in summer and cannot be depended on for water!
Again, God honors Jeremiah's complaint with a reply. It begins with an implied rebuke: *"If you will turn back, I will take you back, and you shall stand before me"* (12:19). Jeremiah had often called on his people to repent and return to God. Now, the Lord calls Jeremiah himself to repent.

"Lord, I'm Between a Rock and a Hard Place!"

Finally, let's take a look at that classic Jeremiah confession in chapter 20. In this conversation with God, Jeremiah expresses some of his own inner conflicts. He was deeply hurt by the ridicule and sarcasm with which his preaching was received by the people. But he could do no other because of his deep commitment to his prophetic vocation. Let's hear Jeremiah in his own words:

If I say, 'I will not mention him, or speak any more in his name,' then within me there is something like a burning fire shut up in my bones; I am weary with holding it in, and I cannot.–Jeremiah 20:9

Here is a man who feels compelled to expose the nation's rejection of the Lord and his covenant. Yet he loved his own people deeply. He's in a bind, and he's vexed that the Lord put him there.

This particular prayer/confession begins with this address to the Lord: *"O Lord, you seduced me, and I was seduced"* (20:7). What! Is Jeremiah expressing the feeling that the Lord deceived him, lured him into the prophetic role, and then tossed him aside? The language borders on the blasphemous! Is he openly challenging his calling? Read Jeremiah 20:7-9 for yourself and see if Jeremiah's outburst is not tantamount to a questioning of the very validity of his call from God.

Later, Jeremiah curses the day he was born! (20:14) To curse either God or one's parents was a capital offense in Israel (Leviticus 20:9; 24:10-16). Jeremiah avoided both by merely cursing the day of his birth. In these verses, Jeremiah plumbs the depths of bitterness and despair, revealing a depth of misery and agony that is not heard from the lips of any other prophet. And remember, *he's saying these things to God.*

What have I learned from Jeremiah's example? I have learned that I can be brazen, shameless, candid, and bold in my prayer life with God. I have no right to be disrespectful or rude. But, I can be honest and share the deepest feelings of my heart with him. Hey, that's what good friends do!

Want to improve your prayer life? Take a page from Jeremiah's prayer journal. Bear your soul to God. Tell him exactly how you feel and what you feel you need. You won't be struck down for it. Rather, you will only draw closer to God and him, to you. You will discover that your friendship with him will only deepen.

BRM No. 6: *Images of the* MASTER

The Bible Reading Marathons began in 2012. In the first BRM, we read through the entire Bible in chronological order. Then, basic Bible themes were explored as we settled on a "topical" reading schedule rather than a chronological plan. This approach made the Marathon more a *study* experience rather than just *reading passages*. We have added notch articles, *Growing Panes,* to focus on various topics related to the Bible. The *Contributors,* or compilers of the passages, are serious Bible students and seasoned mature Christians. Most of them are regular Bible class teachers.

Themes of the Bible Reading Marathons have been:

BRM #1: **Reading through the Bible**
BRM #2: **These Things We Believe**
BRM #3: **Standing on the Promises of God**
BRM #4: **Our God…An Awesome God!**
BRM #5: **Ask…for the Old Paths**
And, now
BRM #6: **Images of the Master**

The theme this year includes everything the Apostle of John wrote in the Bible, i.e., *The Gospel of John, 1st 2nd* and *3rd John* and the *Book of Revelation.* These passages will outline a detailed set of Scriptures that expand, illustrate and comment on the images of Jesus from the words of John. This year's BRM will let the Bible interpret the Bible!

When the current Bible Reading Marathon is completed, over the course of six years those who ran the *FAST TRACK* will have read more than 60,000 verses of Scripture! Since it takes from ten to fifteen hours for the *Contributors* to read and select the passages, that amounts to between 1500-2000 man (woman) hours of preparation! In total that translates into nearly a full year of 40-hour-work weeks. Have a blessed "run" with John, the Apostle of love.

Make the Commitment!

The Bible Reading Marathon is designed for the young Bible reader as well as the more mature experienced student of God's Word. And, it includes all of us who are in between these two! Just select the "lane" you wish to run and make the commitment to read regularly.

☐ ⇒The *INSIDE TRACK* is for those who choose to read short passages of Scripture.
☐ ⇒The *MIDDLE LANES* schedule readings that summarize the topic of the week with narratives and longer passages of Scripture. Most runners will exercise in the *MIDDLE LANES.*
☐ ⇒For those who are really serious about developing a regular habit of Bible reading, the *FAST TRACK* requires the most time and discipline. If you take the *FAST TRACK* you will read all the Scriptures in the *INSIDE TRACK,* the *MIDDLE LANES* **and** the *FAST TRACK!*

I want to join others in this spiritual exercise by entering the 6th BRM. I hereby promise that I will dedicate the time and the effort to finish the race. If I get behind, or temporarily drop out, I understand that all I have to do is just re-enter at the current reading. (I also understand that others may enter the race on any given Sunday after it has started.)

A weekly progress report may be given every Sunday morning, or, if you are out of town, call the church office and report that you are up-to-date on the readings.

_____
(signed/Date)

The Power of Love

Back in the fifteenth century, in a village near Nuremberg, Germany lived a family with eighteen children. The father and head of the household, a goldsmith by profession, worked almost eighteen hours a day at his trade and any other paying chore he could find in the neighborhood.

Despite their seemingly hopeless condition, two of Albrecht Durer the Elder's children had a dream to pursue their talent for art; however, they knew full well that their father would never be financially able to send them to study at the Academy.

After many long discussions at night in their crowded bed, the two boys finally worked out a pact. They would toss a coin. The loser would go down into the nearby mines and, with his earnings, support his brother while he attended the academy. Then, when that brother who won the toss completed his studies, in four years, he would support the other brother at the academy, either with sales of his artwork or, if necessary, also by laboring in the mines.

They tossed a coin on a Sunday morning after church. Albrecht Durer the younger won the toss and went off to Nuremberg. Albert went down into the dangerous mines and, for the next four years, financed his brother, whose work at the academy was almost an immediate sensation.

Albrecht's etchings, his woodcuts, and his oils were far better than those of most of his professors, and by the time he graduated, he was beginning to earn considerable fees for his commissioned works.

When the young artist returned to his village, the Durer family held a festive dinner on their lawn to celebrate Albrecht's triumphant homecoming.

After a long and memorable meal, punctuated with music and laughter, Albrecht rose from his honored position at the head of the table to drink a toast to his beloved brother for the years of sacrifice that had enabled Albrecht to fulfill his ambition. His closing words were, "And now, Albert, blessed brother of mine, now it is your turn. Now you can go to Nuremberg to pursue your dream, and I will take care of you."

All heads turned in eager expectation to the far end of the table where Albert sat, tears streaming down his pale face, shaking his lowered head from side to side while he sobbed and repeated, over and over, "No ...no ...no ...no."

Finally, Albert rose and wiped the tears from his cheeks. He glanced down the long table at the faces he loved, and then, holding his hands close to his right cheek, he said softly, "No, brother. I cannot go to Nuremberg. It is too late for me. Look ... look what four years in the mines have done to my hands! The bones in every finger have been smashed at least once, and lately I have been suffering from arthritis so badly in my right hand that I cannot even hold a glass to return your toast, much less make delicate lines on parchment or canvas with a pen or a brush.

"No, brother ... for me it is too late."

One day, to pay homage to Albert, Albrecht Durer painstakingly drew his brother's abused hands with palms together and thin fingers stretched skyward. He called his powerful drawing simply "Hands," but the entire world almost immediately opened their hearts to his great masterpiece and renamed his tribute of love "The Praying Hands."

The next time you see a copy of that touching creation, take a second look. Let it be your reminder how powerful love is, and that no one ...*no one* ever makes it alone!

Author Unknown

When God Became a Man
John 1:1 — John 2:18

	INSIDE TRACK	MIDDLE LANES	FAST TRACK
Monday: God Became a Man	☐ John 1:1	☐ John 1:2-18 ☐ Philippians 2:6-11 ☐	☐ Hebrews 1:1-14 ☐ Isaiah 9:5-7 ☐ Matthew 1:1-23 ☐ Matthew 3:1-17 ☐ Galatians 3:23-29
Tuesday: Presented by John the Baptizer	☐ John 1:29	☐ John 1:19-34 ☐ Luke 3:3-16 ☐ Isaiah 40:3-11	☐ Mark 1:9-11 ☐ Hebrews 2:14-18 ☐ Isaiah 42:1-9 ☐ Acts 11:1-18 ☐
Wednesday: Presented to John's Disciples	☐ John 1:36	☐ John 1:35-51 ☐ Hebrews 12:1-3 ☐ Matthew 4:18-23	☐ Proverbs 8:17-36 ☐ Isaiah 61:1-3 ☐ Matthew 16:17-20 ☐ Luke 4:22-30 ☐
Thursday: First Sign Presented in Galilee	☐ John 2:11	☐ John 2:1-12 ☐ Mark 7:3-5 ☐	☐ Matthew 12:46-50 ☐ 1 Corinthians 7:39-40 ☐ Romans 7:2-3 ☐ ☐
Friday: Faith Lessons for Today	☐ Isaiah 53:2	☐ Psalm 22:6-23 ☐ Hebrews 5:8-14 ☐ Luke 24:1-8	☐ Acts 8:32-40 ☐ Luke 24:13-48 ☐ Acts 1:1-11 ☐ Acts 2:22-38 ☐ Matthew 17:1-9

Preacher's Stories - No. 1

West Texas was in the grips of a major dust bowl. Then on top of that, swarms of locusts descended on the small patches of green grass that was left and were devouring it. Every rancher in the area was being threatened with bankruptcy because of the locust invasion. Times were *really* bad!

One of the largest ranchers came into town and was seen at the general store whistling and smiling as he selected a few staples. A neighboring fellow-rancher walked over to him and asked:

"How are you doing?" as he credulously watched the smile on his neighbor's face.

"I'm doing great!" he answered with more optimism than circumstances seem to merit, "We serve a wonderful God!"

"But," continued the neighboring rancher, "Do you have any locusts in your fields?"

"Sure do...swarms of them! Eating up every blade of grass left."

"But...I don't understand," replied the friend, "how can you be so cheerful?"

"Well, here's the way I see it, when I became a Christian, I gave myself and all that I possess to the Lord. And, if he wants to pasture *His* locusts on *His* fields, that's *His* business."

Growing Panes
No. 6-1

Building Belief in God's Son

John 2:13 — John 4:26

	INSIDE TRACK	MIDDLE LANES	FAST TRACK
Monday: Christ Cleansing the Worship Place	☐ John 2:19	☐ John 2:13-25 ☐ Psalm 69:6-9 ☐ Luke 2:41-52	☐ Matthew 21:12-17 ☐ Mark 11:15-19 ☐ Luke 19:45-48 ☐ Mark 14:58-62 ☐ Isaiah 56:1-8
Tuesday: Nicodemus and the New Birth	☐ John 3:5	☐ John 3:1-9 ☐ 1 Peter 1:3-9 ☐	☐ Ezekiel 36:22-28 ☐ Matthew 22:15-22 ☐ Acts 2:36-40 ☐ Acts 10:34-43 ☐ Romans 6:1-11
Wednesday: Belief and Eternal Life	☐ John 3:16	☐ John 3:10-21 ☐ Numbers 21:6-10 ☐ Romans 5:6-11	☐ Romans 8:31-38 ☐ Ephesians 4:1-10 ☐ Psalm 68:17-19 ☐ Ephesians 5:1-14 ☐ Psalm 119:105-112
Thursday: Belief and Worship	☐ John 4:24	☐ John 4:1-26 ☐ Joshua 24:32 ☐ Exodus 34:12-17	☐ Genesis 33:18-20 ☐ Genesis 34:1-2,25-31 ☐ Joshua 24:14-28 ☐ Ezra 4:1-16 ☐ Acts 10:44-48
Friday: Faith Lessons for Today	☐ 1 Corinthians 3:16-17	☐ 1 Corinthians 6:12-20 ☐ Titus 2:11-14 ☐ Titus 3:4-7	☐ 1 Peter 2:13-17 ☐ Ephesians 4:17-32 ☐ Romans 3:21-26 ☐ 2 Timothy 2:21-24 ☐ Philippians 1:27-29

Preacher's Stories - No. 2

Five-year-old Susie was entering the hospital for the first time ever to have her tonsils removed. Both she and her mother were more than a little fearful about it all.

"She's in good hands," assured the nurse, "I will take good care of her!"

The mother left to go home with the assurance that her little daughter was safely in the hands of a trained professional who would take care of her. The frightened little girl was placed in a private room to wait as preparations were made for her surgery.

The nurse got busy with other things and for a time forgot about the little girl. Thinking about her, she decided to call her on the intercom to make sure she was all right.

"Hello Susie," she said over the intercom, "Are you all right?"... *No answer*!...again, she called...still no answer!

"*Little girl...LITTLE GIRL...ARE YOU ALL RIGHT!*" *the nervous nurse shouted into the intercom, "Answer me!"*

Finally, a small trembling voice could be heard from the corner of the room,

"*What do you want, ... wall?*"

Growing Panes

No. 6-2

Many Believed in Jesus

John 4:27– John 4:54

	INSIDE TRACK	MIDDLE LANES	FAST TRACK
Monday: His Disciples Believed	☐ John 4:34	☐ John 4:27-38 ☐ Matthew 11:25-30 ☐ Mark 9:30-40	☐ Mark 16:14-20 ☐ Romans 10:8-15 ☐ Matthew 16:13-20 ☐ Luke 9:1-6,10-27 ☐ Luke 10:1-24
Tuesday: The Samaritans Believed	☐ John 4:41	☐ John 4:39-42 ☐ 2 Kings 17:24-29,41 ☐ Luke 9:51-56	☐ Matthew 9:35-38 ☐ Luke 17:11-19 ☐ Matthew 10:5-15 ☐ Acts 1:4-9 ☐ Acts 8:1-8
Wednesday: The Galileans Believed	☐ John 4:44	☐ John 4:43-45 ☐ Mark 1:14-15 ☐ Matthew 4:12-17	☐ Isaiah 9:1-7 ☐ Luke 4:14-15 ☐ Luke 4:31-44 ☐ Acts 2:1-8 ☐ Mark 14:66-72
Thursday: Second Sign: A Nobleman Believed	☐ John 4:53	☐ John 4:46-54 ☐ Matthew 8:5-13 ☐ Luke 8:1-3	☐ Luke 7:1-10 ☐ 1 Corinthians 1:26-31 ☐ Luke 18:18-30 ☐ Matthew 27:57-60 ☐ Isaiah 53:7-9
Friday: Faith Lessons for Today	☐ Psalm 117:1-2	☐ Acts 10:28-29 ☐ Romans 5:1-11 ☐ Psalm 32:8-11	☐ Acts 10:34-48 ☐ Acts 11:1-4,15-18 ☐ Luke 17:1-10 ☐ James 2:14-26 ☐ Acts 16:23-34

Preacher's Stories –No.3

The man dressed up as Satan for a costume party. He wore the red suit with a flowing red cape. The red face paint and the forked tail really added to his disguise. Since the party was only a few blocks from his home, he decided to walk.

However, as he walked down the street it started to rain. Fearing that his costume would be ruined, he darted into the first open doorway to find shelter. And, as fate would have it, it was a church!

Just as he stepped in out of the rain, the preacher was in the pulpit passionately preaching about the evils of sin.

"If the Devil walked in that door right now, some of you would not change!" he shouted.

About that time, the man walked in ...devil's suit and all. Everyone headed for the windows, including the preacher.

Except for a rather large hysterical lady who was having trouble getting out between the pews.

"It'll be okay...it'll be okay"..the man said walking up to her, trying to calm her down. She just kept backing out of the pew, screaming.

"I want you to know, I've been a member of this church for twenty-five years, *but I've been on your side all the time!*"

Growing Panes

No. 6-3

Francine was 8 years old in 1947 when she came to the Central Avenue church of Christ for the first time. She described how it happened like this:

"Dad was dropping me off at the Smithland Place door to the Sunday school department of the Lee Street Baptist Church. Uncle Len (Samuel Leonard Dowling, a Central Avenue member) suggested to Dad that he drop me off in front of the Central church building instead. The very next day that is what he did. I walked into the old stucco building right by myself not knowing anyone else there."

Subsequently, her mother and her sister Audrey were baptized. Later, sisters Verdie Mae and Iva became Christians along with their husbands, Ed Carter and Donald Parker. Other relatives that followed were "Uncle" Walter Jones (and his wife, Lila), Aunt Ruby Jones (and her daughters, Hazel and Frances). Ed Carter also baptized his next-door neighbor, Earl Jack Wilkerson, who became a preacher and missionary baptizing hundreds more. Ed also made several mission trips to New Zealand. Orrie, Francine's husband, was baptized in 1958 by Jack McElroy. Brother McElroy was killed in a car wreck later that same year. Joel Peters was the last of Francine's brothers-in-law to be baptized.

It had been more than fifteen years since her Uncle Len Dowling suggested to her dad that he drop Francine off on Central Avenue rather than Smithland Place for Sunday school. That simple act had resulted in hundreds of people becoming Christians. The final results in the kingdom of God will not be known until the Judgment. But Francine has expressed some of the joy we feel when people we love become disciples of Christ:

"In 1961 (while I was Joe Gray's secretary), Joe went out to my dad's house and told him it was time. Dad agreed with him and let him baptize him that day. I was so proud when I got to see Dad serving the Lord's supper at Central. A few months later, in October of 1961, he died."

Samuel Leonard Dowling, "Uncle Len", was directly and indirectly responsible for countless new members to the Lord's body. The influence of Jesus on earth, as disciples in the flesh , was greatly enhanced because of him.

Jesus said, "Very truly I tell you no one can see the kingdom of God unless they are born again (John 3:3)." Francine has given us several examples of the word becoming flesh through the spiritual birth. All from a simple invitation to drop off a little girl for Sunday school at the door of the Lord's church rather than at the Sunday school door next door.

Jesus went further: "Very truly I tell you, no one can enter the kingdom of God unless they are born of water and the Spirit (John 3:5)." Coming to church (the assembling of the saints) simply gives individuals the opportunity to hear the soul saving message of Christ. When those individuals are baptized, they become a part of the Body of Christ on earth to bring about more births of the water and the Spirit. One in this chain of converts became a missionary and evangelist for the Body of Christ. All of them became actively involved in the Lord's Body.

Opposition to Belief in Jesus
John 5:1—47

	INSIDE TRACK	MIDDLE LANES	FAST TRACK
Monday: Third Sign: Healing Paralytic Man	☐ John 5:9	☐ John 5:1-9 ☐ Matthew 4:23-25 ☐ Mark 2:1-12	☐ Luke 5:12-26 ☐ Matthew 11:1-6 ☐ Acts 9:32-35 ☐ Acts 14:8-18 ☐ Psalm 103:1-5
Tuesday: Religious Leaders in Opposition	☐ John 5:16	☐ John 5:10-18 ☐ Matthew 22:15-22 ☐ Mark 8:11-13	☐ Matthew 12:1-14 ☐ Mark 3:20-30 ☐ Luke 6:6-11 ☐ Luke 20:19-26 ☐ Matthew 26:1-5
Wednesday: Equality with God Questioned	☐ John 5:22,23	☐ John 5:19-30 ☐ Matthew 4:1-4 ☐ Matthew 26:59-66	☐ Mark 11:27-33 ☐ Mark 14:53-65 ☐ Philippians 2:1-11 ☐ Acts 7:51-60 ☐ 2 Corinthians 4:1-6
Thursday: Witnesses for Jesus	☐ John 5:36	☐ John 5:31-47 ☐ Matthew 3:13-17 ☐ Acts 4:32-35	☐ Acts 9:19b-22 ☐ Acts 1:6-26 ☐ Acts 10:34-43 ☐ Acts 13:26-43 ☐ Matthew 27:45-54
Friday: Faith Lessons for Today	☐ Mark 9:23	☐ Daniel 12:1-4 ☐ Galatians 3:23-29 ☐ Ephesians 2:1-10	☐ 2 Timothy 2:1-13 ☐ I Peter 1:3-9 ☐ Romans 4:1-25 ☐ James 2:14-26 ☐ Philippians 4:4-14

Preacher's Stories -No.4

A couple had two little boys, ages 8 and 10, who were excessively mischievous. The two were always getting into trouble and their parents could be assured that if any mischief occurred in their town their two young sons were in some way involved.

The parents were at their wits end as to what to do about their sons' behavior. The mother had heard that a preacher in town had been successful in disciplining children in the past, so she asked her husband if he thought they should send the boys to speak with the minister.

The husband said, 'We might as well. We need to do something before I really lose my temper!' The minister agreed to speak with the boys, but asked to see them individually. The 8 year old went to meet with him first. The preacher sat the boy down and asked him sternly,'Where is God?'

The boy made no response, so the preacher repeated the question in an even sterner tone, 'Where is God?' Again the boy made no attempt to answer. So the preacher raised his voice even more and shook his finger in the boy's face, 'WHERE IS GOD?'

At that the boy bolted from the room and ran directly home, slamming himself in the closet. His older brother followed him into the closet and asked what had happened.

The younger brother replied, "We are in BIG trouble this time. God is missing and they think we did it."

Growing Panes

No. 6-4

Opposition and Discipleship
John 6:1-71

	INSIDE TRACK	MIDDLE LANES	FAST TRACK
Monday: Fourth Sign: Feeding 5000	☐ John 6:14	☐ John 6:1-14 ☐ Matthew 15:32-39 ☐ 2 Kings 4:42-44	☐ Matthew 16:5-12 ☐ Luke 9:10-17 ☐ Matthew 14:13-21 ☐ Matthew 6:25-33 ☐ Mark 6:30-44
Tuesday: Fifth Sign: Walking on Water	☐ John 6:20	☐ John 6:15-21 ☐ Psalm 107:23-30 ☐ Matthew 8:23-27	☐ Matthew 14:22-33 ☐ Mark 6:45-52 ☐ Hebrews 12:1-2 ☐ James 1:2-12 ☐ Matthew 21:18-22
Wednesday: Claim: "I Am the Bread of Life"	☐ John 6:29	☐ John 6:22-59 ☐ Exodus 16:1-31 ☐ Matthew 4:1-4	☐ 1 Corinthians 5:6-8 ☐ 1 Corinthians 10:14-18 ☐ Luke 22:14-20 ☐ Deuteronomy 8:1-5 ☐ Isaiah 55:1-3
Thursday: Rejection by the Disciples	☐ John 6:67,68	☐ John 6:60-71 ☐ Zechariah 11:12-13 ☐ Matthew 27:3-10	☐ Mark 14:12-21 ☐ Mark 14:26-31 ☐ Mark 14:32-42 ☐ Mark 14:43-50 ☐ Mark 14:66-72
Friday: Faith Lessons for Today	☐ Matthew 5:16	☐ Matthew 5:13-16 ☐ Matthew 10:37-42 ☐ Matthew 28:16-20	☐ Ephesians 5:1-2 ☐ Colossians 3:23-24 ☐ 2 Corinthians 11:24-33 ☐ Philippians 1:27-30 ☐ 2 Timothy 3:10-17

Preacher's Stories – No.5

A doctor, a lawyer, a little boy and a minister were out for a Sunday afternoon flight on a small private plane. Suddenly, the plane developed engine trouble. In spite of the best efforts of the pilot, the plane started to go down. Finally, the pilot grabbed a parachute, yelled to the passengers that they had better jump, and then he bailed out.

Unfortunately, there were only three parachutes remaining. The doctor grabbed one and said "I'm a doctor, I save lives, so I must live," and jumped out.

The lawyer then said, "I'm a lawyer and lawyers are the smartest people in the world. I deserve to live." He also grabbed a parachute and jumped.

The minister looked at the little boy and said, "My son, I've lived a long and full life. You are young and have your whole life ahead of you. Take the last parachute and live in peace."

The little boy handed the parachute back to the minister and said, "Not to worry. The 'smartest man in the world' just took off with my back pack."

Growing Panes

No. 6-5

Growing Opposition to Christ

John 7:1-53

	INSIDE TRACK	MIDDLE LANES	FAST TRACK
Monday: From His Own Family	☐ John 7:12	☐ John 7:1-13 ☐ Leviticus 23:33-34 ☐	☐ Isaiah 52:13-15 ☐ Isaiah 53:1-12 ☐ Mark 6:1-6 ☐ Matthew 26:21-25 ☐
Tuesday: Because He was God's Son	☐ John 7:24	☐ John 7:14-36 ☐ Luke 11:39-54 ☐ Matthew 12:38-41	☐ Luke 7:36-50 ☐ Luke 11:23-28 ☐ Luke 12:51-53 ☐ Matthew 12:42-50 ☐
Wednesday: Because of His Teachings	☐ John 7:37,38	☐ John 7:37-44 ☐ Luke 11:13-20 ☐ Matthew 15:1-9	☐ Matthew 12:1-14 ☐ Matthew 15:10-20 ☐ Mark 14:1-9 ☐ Matthew 19:3-12 ☐
Thursday: From the Jewish Leaders	☐ John 7:43	☐ John 7:45-53 ☐ Mark 11:27-33 ☐ Matthew 20:17-19	☐ Mark 12:12-27 ☐ Luke 19:41-48 ☐ Mark 3:6-12 ☐ Luke 13:10-21 ☐ Mark 14:10-11
Friday: Faith Lessons for Today	☐ Luke 12:4	☐ Luke 4:17-21 ☐ ☐	☐ Matthew 7:15-20 ☐ Romans 3:21-31 ☐ Romans 5:6-11 ☐ ☐

Preacher's Stories -No.6

An elderly woman had just returned to her home from an evening of religious service when she was startled by an intruder.

As she caught the man in the act of robbing her home of its valuables, she yelled, 'Stop -Acts 2:38!' (..turn from your sin...). The burglar stopped dead in his tracks. The woman calmly called the police and explained what she had done.

As the officer cuffed the man to take him in, he asked the burglar, 'Why did you just stand there? All she did was yell a scripture to you.' 'Scripture?' replied the burglar, 'She said she had an AXE and two 38's!'

An atheist was spending a quiet day fishing when suddenly his boat was attacked by the Loch Ness monster. In one easy flip, the beast tossed him and his boat high into the air. Then it opened its mouth to swallow both.

As the man sailed head over heels, he cried out, 'Oh, my God! Help me!'

At once, the ferocious attack scene froze in place, and as the atheist hung in mid-air, a booming voice came down from the clouds, 'I thought you didn't believe in Me!'

Come on God, give me a break!!' the man pleaded. 'Two minutes ago I didn't believe in the Loch Ness monster either!'

Growing Panes

No. 6-6

Believers & Opposition
John 8:1 — John 9:41

DATES
_____ TO _____

INSIDE TRACK	MIDDLE LANES	FAST TRACK

Monday: Woman Caught in Adultery

- ☐ John 8:7
- ☐ John 8:1-11
- ☐ Matthew 18:23-35
- ☐ Colossians 3:12-14
- ☐ Genesis 50:15-21
- ☐ Deuteronomy 22:22-24
- ☐ Luke 6:37-38
- ☐ 2 Corinthians 2:5-11
- ☐ Ephesians 4:1-6

Tuesday: Jesus: The Light of the World

- ☐ John 8:12
- ☐ John 8:12-30
- ☐ Matthew 5:14-16
- ☐ Matthew 27:51-54
- ☐ Deuteronomy 19:15-21
- ☐ Ezekiel 3:16-21
- ☐ Matthew 11:25-30
- ☐ Philippians 2:14-18
- ☐ James 4:4-10

Wednesday: Who is "Your" Father?

- ☐ John 8:32
- ☐ John 8:31-59
- ☐ Leviticus 24:13-16
- ☐ Galatians 5:13-15
- ☐ Exodus 3:7-15
- ☐ Isaiah 64:8-12
- ☐ Matthew 13:10-17
- ☐ Mark 3:20-32
- ☐ Romans 6:15-18

Thursday: Sixth Sign: The Blind will See

- ☐ John 9:11
- ☐ John 9:1-41
- ☐ Ezekiel 18:19-20
- ☐ Nehemiah 3:15-16
- ☐ Psalm 34:15-18
- ☐ Isaiah 35:5-7
- ☐ Matthew 12:1-14
- ☐ Romans 2:17-24
- ☐ James 5:13-18

Friday: Faith Lessons for Today

- ☐ Mark 12:28-31
- ☐ Psalm 119:73-80
- ☐ Romans 12:1-21
- ☐ 2 Corinthians 3:4-6
- ☐ Matthew 5:17-20
- ☐ Galatians 3:1-29
- ☐ 1 Timothy 6:6-10
- ☐ James 2:1-12
- ☐ 1 Peter 2:9-10

Preacher's Stories -No.7

There was a Scottish tradesman, a painter called Jack, who was very interested in making it where he could. So he often would thin down his paint to make it go a wee bit further. As it happened, he got away with this for some time.

Eventually the local church decided to do a big restoration job. Jack put in a painting bid and because his price was so competitive, he got the job.

And so he set to, with a right good will, erecting the trestles and putting up the planks, and buying the paint and...yes, I am sorry to say, thinning it down with the turpentine.

Well, Jack was up on the scaffolding, painting away, the job nearly done, when suddenly there was a horrendous clap of thunder. The sky opened and the rain poured down, washing the thin paint off the building and knocking Jack off the scaffold to land on the lawn below.

Now, Jack was no fool.

He knew this was a judgment from the Almighty, so he fell on his knees and cried,

'Oh, God! Forgive me! What should I do?'

And from the thunder, a mighty Voice spoke,

'Repaint you thinner, And go and thin no more!'

Growing Panes
No. 6-7

God's Watchful Eye

My prayer is not that you take them out of the world but that you protect them from the evil one. John 17:15

God's watchful eye was on little twelve-year-old Rachel when she literally felt the gaze of a predator's evil eyes. She was walking alone on the desolate Sunday-afternoon downtown streets of Valdosta near the courthouse square. In 1949 all the businesses were closed on Sundays; no one was on the streets. Except for a man in a car that drove slowly by her and kept circling the courthouse square, watching her every move!

Rachel was walking from the house of a friend to where her brother worked for Southern Railroads. She was going to ride with him the rest of the way home. She wasn't usually afraid to walk the two miles to the depot, but this time was different. She states:

> "Because this man kept driving around and around the courthouse square, she felt certain that the man planned to stop and force her into his car. Was she afraid? Oh yes, very much so. She wanted to hide, but where? All the stores were closed on Sundays. Who could she scream to for help? NO ONE. The downtown streets were empty of everyone, except Rachael, a twelve-year-old girl and that man in the vehicle that was pursuing her."

While the predator continued circling her and watching and keeping his eyes on her every move, she remembered a small shop across the street from the courthouse that had a kind of indention up to the entrance door. She ran to that shop and crouched down low against the cold cement. The man drove slowly around a few more times, but had lost sight of her, so he then drove away. She felt relief...but she still had to walk quite a bit further to meet her brother at three o'clock! Her fears subsided some, but she still remembers the fear:

> "That fearful episode stayed in my mind for a long time and occasionally is thought of even today many years later. Truthfully, I don't remember if as a 12-year-old girl I thought that God protected and saved me from being abducted, raped and murdered, but I am sure **now**, it was HE!

A wonderful Savior is Jesus my Lord,
A wonderful Savior to me;
He hideth my soul in the cleft of the rock,
Where rivers of pleasure I see.

He hideth my soul in the cleft of the rock,
That shadows a dry, thirsty land;
He hideth my life in the depths of His love,
And covers me there with His hand,
And covers me there with His hand.

A wonderful Savior is Jesus my Lord,
He taketh my burden away,
He holdeth me up and I shall not be moved,
He giveth me strength as my day.

He hideth my soul in the cleft of the rock,
That shadows a dry, thirsty land;
He hideth my life in the depths of His love,
And covers me there with His hand,
And covers me there with His hand.

With numberless blessings each moment He crowns,
And filled with His fullness divine,
I sing in my rapture, oh, glory to God!
For such a Redeemer as mine.

He hideth my soul in the cleft of the rock,
That shadows a dry, thirsty land;
He hideth my life in the depths of His love,
And covers me there with His hand,
And covers me there with His hand.

When clothed with His brightness transported I rise
To meet Him in clouds of the sky,
His perfect salvation, His wonderful love,
I'll shout with the millions on high.

He hideth my soul in the cleft of the rock,
That shadows a dry, thirsty land;
He hideth my life in the depths of His love,
And covers me there with His hand,
And covers me there with His hand.

Hymn by Frances J. Crosby, 1890

Good Shepherd or A Demon?
John 10:1 — John 11:57

	INSIDE TRACK	**MIDDLE LANES**	**FAST TRACK**
Monday: "I Am the Good Shepherd"	☐ John 10:9	☐ John 10:1-18 ☐ Psalm 23:1-6 ☐ Psalm 78:70-72	☐ Matthew 25:31-46 ☐ Matthew 26:26-46 ☐ Mark 14:26-31 ☐ Luke 2:1-21 ☐ Acts 20:17-38
Tuesday: Division, Blasphemy and Demons	☐ John 10:26,27	☐ John 10:19-42 ☐ Ephesians 4:1-16 ☐ Matthew 8:28-34	☐ Matthew 12:22-32 ☐ Titus 3:1-11 ☐ Proverbs 6:1-7 ☐ Proverbs 6:12-19 ☐ James 2:14-26
Wednesday: Seventh Sign: The Dead Raised	☐ John 11:35	☐ John 11:1-44 ☐ Hebrews 9:23-28 ☐ Matthew 27:45-53	☐ Matthew 11:1-6 ☐ Matthew 17:1-9 ☐ Mark 6:14-29 ☐ Matthew 10:5-8 ☐ Acts 10:39-43
Thursday: Plans to Kill Jesus	☐ John 11:47,48	☐ John 11:45-57 ☐ Matthew 26:1-5 ☐ Mark 14:1-11	☐ Matthew 12:9-14 ☐ Mark 3:1-6 ☐ Luke 22:1-23 ☐ Acts 4:8-11 ☐ Acts 3:22-30
Friday: Faith Lessons for Today	☐ John 3:16-17	☐ Romans 10:14-17 ☐ 2 Corinthians 5:1-10 ☐ Luke 12:41-48	☐ Hebrews 6:1-12 ☐ Hebrews 10:19-39 ☐ Titus 2:1-15 ☐ Matthew 5:13-16 ☐

Preacher's Stories - No.8

A little old Christian lady lived next door to an atheist. Every morning the lady came out onto her front porch and shouted

"*Praise the Lord!*"

The atheist then would yell back,

"*There is no God!*"

She would do this every morning with the same result. As time went on the lady ran into financial difficulties and had trouble buying food.

As her custom was, she went out on the porch and asked God for help with groceries, then said "Praise the Lord!"

The next morning she went out on the porch and found the groceries she had asked for. Of course she said "Praise the Lord!" The atheist jumped out from behind a bush and said,

"Ha, I bought those groceries - there is no God!"

The lady looked at him and smiled, then shouted

"Praise the Lord ---

...not only did you provide for me, Lord, you made Satan pay for the groceries!"

°Growing Panes

No. 6-8

Jesus: King of Kings
John 12:1—50

	INSIDE TRACK	MIDDLE LANES	FAST TRACK
Monday: King of Kings Anointed	☐ John 12:7,8	☐ John 12:1-11 ☐ Psalm 2:1-12 ☐ Acts 4:23-31	☐ Matthew 26:6-13 ☐ Mark 16:1-8 ☐ Luke 7:36-50 ☐ Acts 10:34-38 ☐ Hebrews 1:1-9
Tuesday: The Triumphal Entry	☐ John 12:12,13	☐ John 12:12-22 ☐ Psalm 33:1-8 ☐ Zechariah 9:9-17	☐ Psalm 47:1-9 ☐ Luke 9:51-62 ☐ Mark 10:32-34 ☐ Mark 11:1-10 ☐ Matthew 21:12-17
Wednesday: The Truth about Jesus	☐ John 12:32	☐ John 12:23-41 ☐ Isaiah 9:6-7 ☐ Philippians 2:5-11	☐ Isaiah 53:1-12 ☐ Acts 2:29-36 ☐ Ephesians 1:15-23 ☐ 2 Timothy 2:8-13 ☐ Colossians 2:9-15
Thursday: Believe or be Rejected	☐ John 12:48	☐ John 12:42-50 ☐ 1 Thessalonians 4:13-18 ☐ 1 Peter 2:4-8	☐ Matthew 21:42-44 ☐ Acts 3:17-23 ☐ Acts 4:5-12 ☐ Romans 10:1-13 ☐ 1 Corinthians 1:18-25
Friday: Faith Lessons for Today	☐ Hebrews 11:1-3	☐ Matthew 6:25-34 ☐ Romans 3:21-31 ☐ Galatians 3:19-29	☐ 2 Corinthians 4:13-18 ☐ Galatians 2:15-21 ☐ 1 Timothy 6:6-21 ☐ James 2:14-26 ☐ Jude 1:3-7

Preacher's Stories - No.9

Irene, the church gossip, and self appointed monitor of the church's morals, kept sticking her nose into other people's business.

Several members did not approve of her extra curricular activities, but feared her enough to maintain their silence.

Irene made a mistake, however, when she accused George, a new member, of being an alcoholic after she saw his old blue pickup parked in front of the town's only bar one afternoon.

She emphatically told George, and several others, that everyone seeing it there would know exactly what he was doing.

George, a man of few words, stared at her for a few moments and just turned and walked away.

He didn't explain, defend or deny!

He said nothing!

Later that evening, George quietly parked his blue pickup in front of Irene's house .... walked home .... and left it there....all night!

Growing Panes
No. 6-9

18

Son of Man to Son of God
John 13:1 — John 14:21

	INSIDE TRACK	MIDDLE LANES	FAST TRACK
Monday: Learning to Be Humble	☐ John 13:15	☐ John 13:1-20 ☐ Philippians 2:1-8 ☐ 1 Peter 5:1-7	☐ Romans 12:6-13 ☐ James 4:4-10 ☐ Matthew 23:5-11 ☐ 2 Chronicles 7:11-16 ☐ 2 Corinthians 11:28-33
Tuesday: Judas: The Betrayer	☐ John 13:34,35	☐ John 13:21-35 ☐ John 14:22-31 ☐ Mark 14:10-11	☐ Acts 1:12-26 ☐ Luke 6:12-16 ☐ Matthew 27:3-10 ☐ Psalm 41:4-9 ☐ Luke 22:1-6
Wednesday: Peter: To Deny Christ	☐ John 13:38	☐ John 13:36-38 ☐ Matthew 26:31-35 ☐ Luke 22:31-38	☐ Mark 6:1-6 ☐ Matthew 16:21-28 ☐ Matthew 10:32-42 ☐ 2 Timothy 2:8-14 ☐ 2 Peter 2:1-11
Thursday: Jesus was to Go Away	☐ John 14:15	☐ John 14:1-21 ☐ Psalm 90:1-6 ☐ Luke 5:12-16	☐ Mark 2:35-39 ☐ Matthew 14:22-23 ☐ Colossians 3:1-4 ☐ Luke 21:34-36 ☐ Titus 2:11-14
Friday: Faith Lessons for Today	☐ Hebrews 12:2	☐ Ephesians 2:8-10 ☐ Mark 10:46-52 ☐ James 1:2-4	☐ 1 Timothy 1:12-14 ☐ Matthew 21:18-22 ☐ Romans 12:3-5 ☐ 2 Timothy 4:1-8 ☐ Romans 4:20-25

Preacher's Stories -No.10

One day, an atheist professor who constantly tried to disprove God stood up on a podium in front of his class and said,

"Today, class, I will disprove God! If God really exists, then he will knock me off this podium within 15 minutes!"

The professor then took his watch and started to keep time.

"10 minutes to go God!"

"5 minutes to go God!"

Now a football player was outside the door and heard the teacher counting. When he heard what the teacher was doing, he was furious and waited.

"1 minute left!"

"Well, class, as you can see there is no possible way that I will come off this podium so your God is..."

At that moment the football player came charging in and tackled the professor off the podium and onto the floor. Stunned, the professor stammered, "wh-where did you come from?!"

The football player smirked and replied, *"God was busy so he sent me."*

Growing Panes

No. 6-10

19

Relationships of Believers

John 15:1 – John 16:15

	INSIDE TRACK	MIDDLE LANES	FAST TRACK
Monday: Relationship to Christ	☐ John 15:10	☐ John 15:1-11 ☐ Matthew 22:34-40 ☐ Hebrews 12:1-12	☐ Hebrews 3:7-15 ☐ Ephesians 2:14-18 ☐ 2 Corinthians 11:1-4 ☐ Psalm 63:1-11 ☐ Matthew 6:28-34
Tuesday: Relationship to Each Other	☐ John 15:12	☐ John 15:12-17 ☐ 1 Corinthians 12:12-26 ☐ Acts 4:32-37	☐ Acts 2:40-47 ☐ 1 Peter 1:22-25 ☐ 2 Corinthians 13:5-14 ☐ Colossians 4:1-6 ☐ Psalm 133:1-3
Wednesday: Relationship to the World	☐ John 15:18-19	☐ John 15:18-25 ☐ Philippians 2:14-18 ☐ Matthew 5:11-16	☐ Matthew 28:16-20 ☐ 1 Corinthians 15:50-58 ☐ James 4:1-6 ☐ Ephesians 5:8-21 ☐ 2 Timothy 3:10-17
Thursday: Relationship with the Holy Spirit	☐ John 16:7	☐ John 15:26-16:15 ☐ Galatians 5:16-26 ☐ Acts 1:1-8	☐ Luke 12:8-12 ☐ Romans 8:9-27 ☐ Mark 13:9-13 ☐ Luke 11:5-13 ☐ 2 Peter 1:19-21
Friday: Faith Lessons for Today	☐ Romans 10:16	☐ Hebrews 11:1-10 ☐ Ephesians 2:1-10 ☐ Hebrews 4:14-16	☐ 2 Corinthians 5:16-21 ☐ James 2:14-17 ☐ 2 Peter 1:5-11 ☐ Luke 6:46-49 ☐ Romans 5:1-11

Preacher's Stories – No.11

At the Henry Street Hebrew School, Mr. Goldblatt, the new teacher, finished the day's lesson. It was now time for the usual question period.

"Mr. Goldblatt," announced little Joey, "there's something I can't figure out."

"What's that Joey?" asked Goldblatt.

"Well accordin' to the Bible, the Children of Israel crossed the Red Sea. Right?"

"Right."

"And the Children of Israel beat up the Philistines, right?"

"Er--right."

"And the Children of Israel built the Temple, right?"

"Again, you're right."

"And the Children of Israel fought the Egyptians, and the Children of Israel fought the Romans, and the Children of Israel were always doin' somethin' important. Right?"

"All that is right, too," agreed Goldblatt. "So, what's your question?"

"What I wanna know is this," demanded Joey.

"What were all the grown-ups doin'"?

Growing Panes

No. 6-11

"God Was Not Finished with Me Yet!"

"This sickness will not end in death. No, it is for God's glory so that God's Son may be glorified through it." Now Jesus loved Martha and her sister and Lazarus. So when he heard that Lazarus was sick, he stayed where he was two more days, and then he said to his disciples, "Let us go back to Judea."

John 11:4-7

Rudene was waiting at Shand's Hospital in Gainesville, Florida for surgery. She had been diagnosed with a malignant brain tumor which threatened her life. Like any forty-one-year-old wife and mother, she expected to have many more years of life. Even though she and her family had been faithful members of the Central Avenue Church of Christ for years, she was very apprehensive about the surgery.

The night before the surgery, Rudene's sister-in-law came along with her two children for a visit. Her sister-in-law asked if there was anything she could do for her.

I asked them to pray for me.

Rudene said she still remembers what her sister-in-law said in response to this request,

My sister-in-law told me …"not to worry, that **God was not finished with me yet."**

The surgery lasted for fourteen hours and was successful; however, one side of her face was paralyzed. Additional surgeries were required before she could close her right eye.

Forty-four years later, as an 85-year old senior Christian, Rudene states,

"I am very fortunate to be born at a time my family was attending Central Avenue church of Christ…God has been mighty good to me…that I am still alive."

* * *

Christians may not know what the future holds, but we know who holds the future!

Images of the MASTER   6th BIBLE READING MARATHON

Jesus Prays for Believers

John 16:16 — John 17:26

	INSIDE TRACK	MIDDLE LANES	FAST TRACK
Monday: Predicts His Death & Resurrection	☐ John 16:24	☐ John 16:16-33 ☐ Matthew 16:21-23 ☐ Matthew 28:1-15	☐ Matthew 17:22-23 ☐ Mark 10:32-34 ☐ Luke 18:31-34 ☐ Acts 10:26-41 ☐
Tuesday: Jesus Prays for Himself	☐ John 17:3	☐ John 17:1-5 ☐ Matthew 26:36-46 ☐ Luke 23:44-46	☐ Mark 14:32-42 ☐ Matthew 27:45-53 ☐ Luke 3:21-22 ☐ Philippians 3:1-11 ☐
Wednesday: Jesus Prays for His Apostles	☐ John 17:15	☐ John 17:6-19 ☐ Luke 6:12-16 ☐ Matthew 6:5-15	☐ Luke 22:31-33 ☐ Luke 11:1-13 ☐ Matthew 26:17-30 ☐ Mark 9:14-29 ☐ Mark 11:20-26
Thursday: Jesus Prays for All Believers	☐ John 17:20,21	☐ John 17:20-26 ☐ Luke 10:21-24 ☐ Hebrews 4:14-16	☐ Luke 5:16-26 ☐ Matthew 11:25-30 ☐ Matthew 15:32-39 ☐ Matthew 19:13-15 ☐ Mark 1:35-39
Friday: Faith Lessons for Today	☐ Mark 1:35	☐ Hebrews 5:1-10 ☐ Matthew 7:7-12 ☐ Matthew 9:35-38	☐ Luke 18:1-8 ☐ Hebrews 2:14-18 ☐ Ephesians 5:10-20 ☐ 2 Corinthians 4:13-18 ☐ Philippians 2:5-11

Preacher's Stories – No.12

A young minister was sitting in a restaurant eating lunch. He opened a letter from his mother he just got that morning. As he opened it, a twenty dollar bill fell out.

He thought: "Thanks, mom, I could use that right about now." As he finished his meal, he noticed a beggar outside on the sidewalk leaning against the light post. He thought:

"That fella could probably use the $20 more than I."

So he crossed out the names on the envelope and put the $20 in the envelope and wrote across the top in large letters, "PERSEVERE!"

So as not to make a scene, he put the envelope under his arm and dropped it as he walked past the man. The man picked it up and read the message and smiled.

The next day, while the minister was eating his lunch, the same man tapped him on his shoulder and handed him a big wad of bills.

Surprised, the young preacher asked him what that was for.

The man replied, this is your half of the winnings. "PERSEVERE" came in first in the fourth race at the track yesterday, and he paid 30 to 1.

Growing Panes

No. 6-12

The Arrest and Trials of Jesus
John 18:1-40

DATES
_____ TO _____

	INSIDE TRACK	MIDDLE LANES	FAST TRACK
Monday: The Arrest of Jesus	☐ John 18:10	☐ John 18:1-11 ☐ Matthew 26:1-3 ☐ Luke 23:1-6	☐ Matthew 26:14-16 ☐ Matthew 26:36-56 ☐ Mark 14:10-31 ☐ Luke 22:39-53 ☐
Tuesday: Jewish Trial before Annas	☐ John 18:13-14	☐ John 18:12-24 ☐ Mark 14:50-54 ☐ Luke 11:52-53	☐ Mark 14:55-72 ☐ Acts 4:6-12 ☐ Luke 20:20-26 ☐ ☐
Wednesday: Jewish Trial before Caiaphas	☐ John 18:24	☐ John 18:25-27 ☐ Luke 22:54-62 ☐	☐ Matthew 26:57-75 ☐ Isaiah 53:3-7 ☐ Luke 22:63-71 ☐ Galatians 2:11-16 ☐
Thursday: Roman Trials before Pilate	☐ John 18:28-29	☐ John 18:28-40 ☐ Matthew 27:1-5 ☐	☐ John 19:1-16 ☐ Matthew 27:1-10 ☐ Matthew 27:11-26 ☐ Mark 15:1-15 ☐ Luke 23:7-25
Friday: Faith Lessons for Today	☐ Romans 12:19	☐ Romans 12:19-21 ☐ Luke 6:27-28 ☐ James 1:1-4	☐ 1 Peter 3:13-17 ☐ 1 Corinthians 13:1-7 ☐ Genesis 45:1-8 ☐ Romans 8:28-39 ☐ 2 Corinthians 4:16-18

Preacher's Stories -No.13

There was a young lion who wandered from his father to test whether or not he would get the same respect from the other animals as his father did.

As the young lion approached some monkeys, he roared and asked, "WHO IS THE KING OF THE JUNGLE?" The monkeys, being afraid, responded, "YOU are!" The lion replied, "And don't you forget it!"

The lion repeated this to each animal in the jungle and got the same response until he came across a herd of elephants. The little lion roared and asked, "WHO IS THE KING OF THE JUNGLE?" The big bull elephant walked closer to the lion, swooped him up in his trunk, swung him around and around and threw him in the river.

Battered and wet, the little lion replied, "*Just because you didn't know the answer to the question didn't mean you had to get nasty about it!*"

Most of us roar through life in the same way without God until life throws us in a tail spin and shows us that we are not "king of the jungle."

Growing Panes
No. 6-13

23

His Death and Resurrection
John 19:1 — John 20:10

	INSIDE TRACK	MIDDLE LANES	FAST TRACK
Monday: The Passion of Jesus	☐ John 19:16	☐ John 19:1-16 ☐ Isaiah 53:1-6 ☐ Matthew 27:15-25	☐ Mark 14:53-65 ☐ Mark 15:6-14 ☐ Luke 23:1-25 ☐ Hebrews 10:1-10 ☐
Tuesday: The Crucifixion of Jesus	☐ John 19:19	☐ John 19:17-37 ☐ Psalm 22:16-31 ☐ Mark 15:15-23	☐ Psalm 22:1-15 ☐ Matthew 27:35-44 ☐ Mark 15:24-40 ☐ Luke 23:33-43 ☐ Isaiah 53:7-12
Wednesday: The Burial of Jesus	☐ John 19:41,42	☐ John 19:38-42 ☐ Matthew 27:57-65 ☐ Romans 6:1-4	☐ Matthew 26:6-12 ☐ Mark 14:1-9 ☐ Mark 15:42-47 ☐ Luke 23:50-56 ☐
Thursday: The Resurrection of Jesus	☐ John 20:9,10	☐ John 20:1-10 ☐ Matthew 28:1-8 ☐ Luke 24:1-12	☐ Matthew 28:9-17 ☐ Luke 24:33-43 ☐ Mark 16:1-16 ☐ Acts 2:29-35 ☐ Romans 6:5-14
Friday: Faith Lessons for Today	☐ Colossians 3:1-2	☐ Psalm 16:1-11 ☐ 1 Peter 2:21-25 ☐ 1 Corinthians 15:1-11	☐ 1 Corinthians 2:1-10 ☐ 1 Corinthians 15:12-22 ☐ 2 Corinthians 13:1-9 ☐ Philippians 2:1-11 ☐ Hebrews 12:1-11

Preacher's Stories - No.14

A new Preacher came to his first church, a small old country church. The first Sunday, only one person showed up for the morning service, a little old man in bib-over-alls.

The Preacher said to the man, "Brother, you seem to be the only one to show up this morning, should I preach or what?"

The little old man replied, "Well Sir, I ain't no preacher, I'm just an old farmer, but if I had a truck load of hay, and I went to the pasture and only one cow showed up, I'd feed that cow!"

The Preacher, inspired by these words of wisdom, began to preach like he never had before, he preached every thing he had learned or heard and then began to make up stuff, finally after more than an hour, he finished.

He looked to the little old man and said, "Well brother, what did you think of my first sermon here?"

The little old man replied,

"Well Sir, I ain't no preacher, I'm just a little old farmer, but if I had a truck load of hay and I went to the pasture and only one cow showed up, I wouldn't dump the whole load !"

°Growing Panes
No. 6-14

Appearances of Jesus
John 20:11– John 21:14

	INSIDE TRACK	MIDDLE LANES	FAST TRACK
Monday: To Mary Magdalene	☐ John 20:17	☐ John 20:11-18 ☐ Matthew 28:1-10 ☐ Mark 16:1-11	☐ Luke 23:50-56 ☐ Matthew 27;51-57 ☐ Luke 24:1-11 ☐ Luke 24:13-27 ☐ Ephesians 1:15-20
Tuesday: To the Disciples, except Thomas	☐ John 20:20	☐ John 20:19-25 ☐ Luke 24:36-53 ☐ Matthew 10:12-14	☐ Romans 1:1-7 ☐ Psalm 119: 73-80 ☐ Matthew 18:15-20 ☐ ☐
Wednesday: To the Disciple with Thomas	☐ John 20:27	☐ John 20:26-29 ☐ Matthew 28:16-20 ☐	☐ Acts 3:26-41 ☐ Luke 24:36-53 ☐ 1 Peter 1:5-9 ☐ ☐
Thursday: To the Disciples Again	☐ John 21:6	☐ John 21:1-14 ☐ Matthew 4:18-22 ☐ Mark 1:14-20	☐ Acts 1:1-14 ☐ Mark 16:14-20 ☐ Luke 22:54-62 ☐ 1 Corinthians 15:3-10 ☐
Friday: Faith Lessons for Today	☐ 1 Corinthians 15:1-2	☐ Daniel 7:13-14 ☐ Psalm 16:5-11 ☐ 1 Peter 1:3-8	☐ Acts 2:22-28 ☐ Acts 2:29-39 ☐ Acts 9:1-18 ☐ 1 Corinthians 15:35-49 ☐ 1 Corinthians 15:50-58

Preacher's Stories –No.15

The building was completely full. It was a traditional church with a long and glorious history of serving the Lord. The auditorium was appointed with cushioned pews and beautiful trappings. It was a typical Sunday; regular worshippers dressed in their finest had come again to worship the Lord

The renowned minister had just taken the pulpit when a strange visitor opened the back door and started down the aisle looking for a seat. He was a young man in his early twenties. His long hair and tattooed arms set him apart, but his well-worn raveled jeans made him look almost inappropriate in this gathering.

A gasping silence fell over the entire congregation while they watched him slowly walk all the way to the front looking for a vacant seat. There was none.

So, on one side of the front the young man just dropped to the floor into a cross-legged sitting position. Very proper for a late-night college devo, but very out-of-place here.

About that time, the only sound that could be heard was that of the tapping cane as an elderly Christian rose from his seat and slowly walked down toward the young man. Then, with considerable difficulty, the old man slowly sat down on the floor beside the young visitor.

The stunned preacher broke the silence and said,

"You will soon forget what I say here today, but you will never forget the sermon you have just seen here today!"

Growing Panes
No. 6-15

My Life in God's Hands

It has given me great joy to find some of your children walking in the truth, just as the Father commanded us. And now, dear lady, I am not writing you a new command but one we have had from the beginning. I ask that we love one another. 2 John 1:4-5

Denise was raised in the Lord's church. She had witnessed the love and devotion her mother and daddy had for each other. She saw the love Christians experience both in her family and in her church. But, she was not ready for the shock when her husband left her and their children for another woman. She was frightened, hostile with anger, and emotionally drained as she remembers:

"The children and I had to fend for ourselves. It was devastating for us and was to be a huge adjustment in our lives. I would never have made it without the support from my parents and my faith in God. I was raised in the church, but this was the first time my life was in God's hands."

She was faced with the emotional and spiritual trauma of "DIVORCE." Like most women in such a situation, she felt angry, but also helpless. All the certainties and foundations of her life were challenged and shaken. Now, as a single parent she must provide the economic and emotional support for her children. But, as she looks back on those events that started to unravel in 1996, she and her children not only *survived*, but *thrived!* Looking back, she recounts:

"My children are Christians with their own wonderful families…this made me a stronger person, and a will to be strong for others, (I have even been called "Dear Abby"). Several years ago someone came into my life that needed guidance. Both our lives are much better now with the strengths we share. I feel like God has given a purpose to my life and that is to help others …I always put my trust in God to guide me for patience and love. I look at God as my Best Friend!"

* * *

When the Japanese mend broken objects, they aggrandize the damage by filling the cracks with gold. They believe that when something's suffered damage and has a history it becomes more beautiful. ~Barbara Bloom

	INSIDE TRACK	MIDDLE LANES	FAST TRACK
Monday: John's Faith Lessons	☐ John 20:30-31	☐ John 21:15-25 ☐ Mark 4:35-41 ☐	☐ Mark 6:30-44 ☐ Luke 9:28-36 ☐ Matthew 20:20-28 ☐ Matthew 4:18-22 ☐ Luke 5:1-11
Tuesday: Fellowship with God	☐ 1 John 1:7	☐ 1 John 1:1-2:14 ☐ Genesis 5:22-24 ☐	☐ Genesis 6:5-9 ☐ 2 Corinthians 6:14-18 ☐ ☐ ☐
Wednesday: Do Not Love the World	☐ 1 John 2:15	☐ 1 John 2:15-17 ☐ James 4:1-8 ☐ Matthew 6:19-20	☐ Matthew 6:25-34 ☐ Romans 1:18-32 ☐ Hebrews 11:4-16 ☐ 2 Corinthians 4:1-6 ☐
Thursday: Watch out for the Deceiver	☐ 1 John 2:25,26	☐ 1 John 2:18-27 ☐ 1 Peter 5:8-11 ☐ Ezekiel 13:6-10	☐ Genesis 3:1-13 ☐ Ephesians 6:10-20 ☐ 2 Timothy 2:9-12 ☐ Luke 4:1-13 ☐
Friday: Faith Lessons for Today	☐ 2 Corinthians 11:14	☐ Philippians 3:7-11 ☐ Psalm 119:105-112 ☐ James 4:4-10	☐ Deuteronomy 5:32-33 ☐ Ephesians 2:1-10 ☐ Hebrews 11:32-40 ☐ Matthew 22:34-40 ☐

Preacher's Stories -No.16

*T*he preacher was really "waxing eloquent" as he delivered the eulogy for a departed brother who was well-known by the community.

"Brother Sam was a member of the church, a fellow-traveler whose example will remain in our hearts for years!" the minister said with an air of pride.

"He was an upstanding citizen of this community and was a diligent civil servant" he continued.

"A great father, a loving husband," he asserted.

The preacher summed it up with,

"Ole Sam was just an all-around good guy that will be sorely missed!"

The widow and her three children sat intently listening as the preacher groaned on about what "a great man Sam" had been. Quietly, she leaned over to one of her children and said,

"Go up there and see if that is Pa in that casket."

Growing Panes

No. 6-16

Conditions of Fellowship

1 John 2:28 — 1 John 5:3

	INSIDE TRACK	MIDDLE LANES	FAST TRACK
Monday: Live a Pure Life of Righteousness	☐ 1 John 3:1	☐ 1 John 2:28-3:12 ☐ 1 Corinthians 1:4-9 ☐ Matthew 13:40-43	☐ 2 Corinthians 6:14-18 ☐ Matthew 28:16-20 ☐ 1 Corinthians 5:1-5 ☐ Galatians 5:22-26 ☐ James 4:11-12
Tuesday: Love in Deed and Truth	☐ 1 John 3:18	☐ 1 John 3:13-24 ☐ 1 Corinthians 13:1-13 ☐ Matthew 25:34-40	☐ Matthew 25:41-46 ☐ Hebrews 13:1-3 ☐ Matthew 22:37-40 ☐ James 2:14-17 ☐ Matthew 18:15-20
Wednesday: Test the Spirits	☐ 1 John 4:1	☐ 1 John 4:1-6 ☐ 1 Corinthians 12:1-11 ☐ Philippians 2:1-4	☐ Acts 4:23-31 ☐ Romans 8:1-6 ☐ 1 Corinthians 3:16-17 ☐ Galatians 5:16-18 ☐ Ephesians 5:15-20
Thursday: Love as Christ Loved	☐ 1 John 4:11	☐ 1 John 4:7-5:3 ☐ Romans 5:6-8 ☐	☐ Luke 22:14-23 ☐ Romans 8:28-39 ☐ Ephesians 5:1-2 ☐ ☐
Friday: Faith Lessons for Today	☐ Romans 5:8	☐ Ephesians 5:25-32 ☐ Psalm 133:1-3 ☐ 1 Peter 3:8-12	☐ Acts 2:42-47 ☐ Hebrews 10:19-25 ☐ 2 Peter 3:11-16 ☐ James 5:7-9 ☐

Preacher's Stories - No.17

A mother took her young son to a Paderewski concert to encourage his progress on the piano. After they were seated, the mother spotted a friend in the audience and went to greet her. Seizing the opportunity to explore the wonders of the concert hall, the little boy rose and eventually explored his way through a door marked "NO ADMITTANCE."

When the house lights dimmed and the concert was about to begin, the mother returned to her seat and discovered that the child was missing. Suddenly, the curtains parted and spotlights focused on the Steinway on stage. In horror, the mother saw her little boy was sitting at the keyboard, innocently picking out "Twinkle, Twinkle Little Star."

At that moment, the great piano master made his entrance, quickly moved to the piano, and whispered in the boy's ear, "Don't quit. Keep playing."

Then, with his left hand Paderewski began filling in a bass part, then the obligato. Together, the old master and the young novice transformed a frightening situation into a wonderfully creative experience.

The audience was so mesmerized that they couldn't recall what else the great master played - only the classic "Twinkle, Twinkle Little Star."

Next time you set out to accomplish great feats, listen carefully. You may hear the voice of the Master, whispering in your ear, "Don't quit. Keep playing."

Growing Panes
No. 6-17

Love: Keep His Commandments

1 John 5:4 — Revelation 1:20

DATES
_____ TO _____

	INSIDE TRACK	MIDDLE LANES	FAST TRACK
Monday: Consequences of Loving God	☐ 1 John 5:13	☐ 1 John 5:4-21 ☐ Micah 7:15-20 ☐ Psalm 71:5-19	☐ Isaiah 49:24-25 ☐ Romans 11:25-27 ☐ 2 Thessalonians 3:2 ☐ 2 Samuel 22:2-6 ☐ Psalm 14:1-7
Tuesday: Fellowship in Him	☐ 2 John 1:4	☐ 2 John 1:1-12 ☐ Zechariah 14:7-12 ☐ 2 Chronicles 31:1-10	☐ 2 Chronicles 35:1-6 ☐ Psalm 111:1-10 ☐ Isaiah 41:1-7 ☐ 1 Samuel 30:3-6 ☐ Isaiah 40:9-15
Wednesday: Fellowship with Brothers	☐ 3 John 1:4	☐ 3 John 1:1-14 ☐ Amos 9:9-15 ☐ Psalm 21:1-7	☐ Psalm 103:6-14 ☐ Isaiah 57:14-21 ☐ Joel 2:18-27 ☐ Isaiah 42:1-9 ☐
Thursday: Images of the Master Now	☐ Revelation 1:17,18	☐ Revelation 1:1-20 ☐ Malachi 3:6-12 ☐	☐ Jeremiah 35:12-16 ☐ Psalm 77:11-20 ☐ Ezekiel 34:25-31 ☐ Zechariah 8:12-17 ☐ Psalm 72:1-19
Friday: Faith Lessons for Today	☐ Isaiah 44:22	☐ Isaiah 55:6-13 ☐ Hosea 14:1-4 ☐	☐ Psalm 105:7-15 ☐ Isaiah 10:21-22 ☐ Jeremiah 12:12-22 ☐ ☐

Preacher's Stories - No. 18

If you were to look at Rembrandt's painting of *The Three Crosses,* your attention would be drawn first to the center cross on which Jesus died.

Then as you would look at the crowd gathered around the foot of that cross, you'd be impressed by the various facial expressions and actions of the people involved in the awful crime of crucifying the Son of God.

Finally, your eyes would drift to the edge of the painting and catch sight of another figure, almost hidden in the shadows.

Art critics say this is a representation of Rembrandt himself, for he recognized that by his sins he helped nail Jesus to the cross.

Growing Panes
No. 6-18

	INSIDE TRACK	MIDDLE LANES	FAST TRACK
Monday: The Church in Ephesus	☐ Revelation 2:4	☐ Revelation 2:1-7 ☐ Jeremiah 50:4-7 ☐ Matthew 10:5-8	☐ Ephesians 1:13-23 ☐ Psalm 119:169-176 ☐ Philippians 2:12-16 ☐ Acts 2:43-47 ☐
Tuesday: The Church in Smyrna	☐ Revelation 2:10	☐ Revelation 2:8-11 ☐ 1 Corinthians 4:10-13 ☐ 1 Corinthians 12:23-26	☐ Acts 26:21-23 ☐ Colossians 3:1-6 ☐ Ephesians 5:22-32 ☐ 1 Thessalonians 1:2-4 ☐
Wednesday: The Church in Pergamos	☐ Revelation 2:13	☐ Revelation 2:12-17 ☐ Ruth 1:14-19 ☐ Philippians 2:1-4	☐ Philippians 3:8-11 ☐ 1 Timothy 1:12-17 ☐ Titus 3:3-7 ☐ Matthew 25:1-13 ☐
Thursday: The Church in Thyatira	☐ Revelation 2:19	☐ Revelation 2:18-29 ☐ Colossians 1:13-19 ☐ Colossians 3:5-11	☐ Jude 1:8-19 ☐ Ephesians 5:1-5 ☐ 1 Corinthians 6:15-20 ☐ Galatians 5:19-21 ☐
Friday: Faith Lessons for Today	☐ 1 Thess 4:16-17	☐ 2 Peter 2:4-10 ☐ 1 Peter 5:8-11 ☐ Titus 1:10-14	☐ Jude 1:20-25 ☐ 2 Peter 3:2-13 ☐ Jeremiah 7:1-34 ☐ ☐

Preacher's Stories –No.19

Oswald Golter was a missionary in northern China during the 1940's. After ten years service, he was returning home. His ship stopped in India, and while waiting for a boat home he found a group of refugees living in a warehouse on the pier. Unwanted by anyone else, the refugees were stranded there. Golter went to visit them. As it was Christmas-time, he wished them a merry Christmas and asked them what they would like for Christmas.

"We're not Christians," they said. "We don't believe in Christmas."

"I know," said the missionary, "but what do you want for Christmas?" They described some German pastries they were particularly fond of, and so Oswald Golter cashed in his ticket, used the money to buy baskets and baskets of the pastries, took them to the refugees, and wished them a merry Christmas.

When he later recounted the incident to a class, a student said,

"But sir, why did you do that for them? They weren't Christians. They don't even believe in Jesus."

"I know," he replied, *"but I do!"*

Growing Panes
No. 6-19

The Future Direction of My Life

When I saw him, I fell at his feet as though dead. Then he placed his right hand on me and said: "Do not be afraid. I am the First and the Last. I am the Living One; I was dead, and now look, I am alive for ever and ever! And I hold the keys of death and Hades. Revelation 1:17-18

ohn's life was carefully planned since his early teens. He aspired to be a sports broadcaster with a college degree in journalism. The plan was to attend North Texas State University just north of his home in Dallas, Texas. In addition to being academically sound, since it was a state university it would be economically reasonable in costs.

John set out on this plan completing his first year at NTSU, but things began to change when he moved in to live with his father and step-mother. They attended the Garland Road church of Christ and insisted that he attend with them. After several months, he surprised them late one Sunday night stating that he wanted to be baptized into Christ. During the subsequent months, John noted:

"I started to grow in the Lord…I began studying the Bible and praying to God about the direction of my life, and what God's will might be regarding my major in college…I began considering changing my major to youth ministry…this would necessitate changing to a Christian college…and more expense."

This would be a major change in the direction of John's life. It would mean a transfer to Abilene Christian, with a major increase in costs. He knew that he had to talk with his father about it, but dreaded the meeting. John recounted that meeting like this:

"…it was probably about six in the morning, we both were eating breakfast in the kitchen. For some reason, my dad brought the subject up about my major. I reluctantly broached the subject about my changing my major to youth ministry as well as my changing to Abilene Christian College.

When I finally got the words out of my mouth, my dad, without blinking an eye, said "Your step-mom and I have been praying and talking about that for a long time…You could have knocked me over with a feather."

* * *

Now, 42 years later, John continues on the change of direction he took that morning, with his dad's blessings and support. More than three decades of that ministry has been with the Central Avenue church.

Churches and The Master
Revelation 3:1 – 4:11

	INSIDE TRACK	MIDDLE LANES	FAST TRACK
Monday: The Church at Sardis	☐ Revelation 3:4	☐ Revelation 3:1-6 ☐ Job 34:21-30 ☐ Psalm 14:1-7	☐ 1 Samuel 2:1-10 ☐ Psalm 20:6-9 ☐ Deuteronomy 3:23-25 ☐ Psalm 45:3-9 ☐ Zechariah 9:9-13
Tuesday: The Church at Philadelphia	☐ Revelation 3:11	☐ Revelation 3:7-13 ☐ Matthew 18:15-20 ☐ Matthew 7:7-9	☐ Titus 1:10-16 ☐ 2 Peter 2:1-3 ☐ 1 Thessalonians 5:23-24 ☐ 1 Peter 1:13-16 ☐ 2 Peter 1:16-18
Wednesday: The Church at Laodicea	☐ Revelation 3:16	☐ Revelation 3:14-22 ☐ Zechariah 13:7-9 ☐ 1 Peter 1:3-9	☐ Proverbs 3:11-12 ☐ Jude 1:5-10 ☐ Hebrews 12:4-11 ☐ Proverbs 1:22-27 ☐
Thursday: The Throne of God	☐ Revelation 4:11	☐ Revelation 4:1-11 ☐ Psalm 103:1-22 ☐ Ezekiel 1:1-28	☐ Matthew 3:13-17 ☐ Mark 16:15-20 ☐ Acts 7:54-60 ☐ 2 Corinthians 12:1-10 ☐ Psalm 150:1-6
Friday: Faith Lessons for Today	☐ Matthew 5:3	☐ Matthew 28:16-20 ☐ James 2:14-24 ☐ Galatians 5:19-26	☐ Psalm 104:1-35 ☐ Matthew 5:4-12 ☐ Matthew 5:43-48 ☐ Matthew 6:25-34 ☐

Preacher's Stories - No. 20

Charles Plumb was a jet fighter pilot in Vietnam. After 75 combat missions, his plane was destroyed by a surface-to-air missile. Plumb ejected and parachuted into enemy hands. He was captured and spent six years in a Communist prison. He survived that ordeal and now lectures about lessons learned from that experience.

One day, when Plumb and his wife were sitting in a restaurant, a man at another table came up and said, "You're Plumb! You flew jet fighters in Vietnam from the aircraft carrier Kitty Hawk. You were shot down!"

"How in the world did you know that?" asked Plumb.

"I packed your parachute," the man replied. Plumb gasped in surprise and gratitude. The man pumped his hand and said, "I guess it worked!"

Plumb assured him, "It sure did – if your chute hadn't worked, I wouldn't be here today."

Plumb thought of the many hours the sailor had spent in the bowels of the ship carefully weaving the shrouds and folding the silks of each chute, holding in his hands each time the fate of someone he didn't know.

Now, Plumb asks his audience, "*Who's packing your parachute? Everyone has someone who provides what they need to make it through the day.*"

Growing Panes
No. 6-20

Worthy is the Lamb of God
Revelation 5:1 — Revelation 8:5

	INSIDE TRACK	MIDDLE LANES	FAST TRACK
Monday: The Sealed Book and the Lamb	☐ Revelation 5:5	☐ Revelation 5:1-14 ☐ Isaiah 11:1-10 ☐ Ezekiel 2:9-10	☐ Hebrews 12:22-24 ☐ Hebrews 7:12-16 ☐ Isaiah 53:1-12 ☐ Luke 3:1-6 ☐ Colossians 1:15-20
Tuesday: Six Seals Opened by the Lamb	☐ Revelation 6:9	☐ Revelation 6:1-17 ☐ Zechariah 6:1-7 ☐ Zechariah 1:8-10	☐ Ezekiel 14:18-21 ☐ Hebrews 11:36-40 ☐ Zechariah 14:3-9 ☐ 2 Peter 2:4-10 ☐ Romans 6:10-20
Wednesday: The Saved in White Robes	☐ Revelation 7:13,14	☐ Revelation 7:1-17 ☐ Isaiah 9:7-18 ☐ Isaiah 25:6-9	☐ Jeremiah 49:35-39 ☐ Ezekiel 9:1-7 ☐ Hebrews 9:6-20 ☐ Ephesians 2:1-10 ☐ Romans 5:1-11
Thursday: The Seventh Seal Opened	☐ Revelation 8:4	☐ Revelation 8:1-5 ☐ Ezekiel 10:1-17 ☐ Isaiah 30:27-33	☐ Ezekiel 38:18-23 ☐ Jeremiah 51:20-26 ☐ Isaiah 14:12-20 ☐ Ephesians 6:10-20 ☐
Friday: Faith Lessons for Today	☐ Romans 1:1-6	☐ 1Timothy 2:1-15 ☐ James 5:7-20 ☐ Hebrews 13:7-22	☐ 2 Thessalonians 1:1-12 ☐ 1 Peter 2:1-12 ☐ 2 Timothy 4:1-8 ☐ Colossians 1:9-14 ☐ Philippians 2:1-18

Preacher's Stories -No.21

Lou Gehrig's career was shortened by ALS, a debilitating muscle disease that eventually stops the heart, now known as "Lou Gehrig's Disease.

The New York Yankee fans honored him at his last baseball game as he ended his baseball career. He was asked to speak. What would you have said in the face of this heartbreaking challenge?

Amazingly, he began: *"Today I consider myself the luckiest man on the face of the earth."*

How could he say that? Gratitude. Gratitude for all the gifts he had been given, for all the love he had been shown by fans, for all the opportunities he had. He focused on the joys not the losses. That's cultivating thankfulness!

Being thankful doesn't come easy for some of us, but God says to cultivate thankfulness. How do you cultivate anything? You work at it. You nourish it. You do whatever it takes to make it thrive.

Gratitude comes from humility.

"A proud man is seldom a grateful man, for he never thinks he gets as much as he deserves" (Henry Ward Beecher).

A Christian truly is the luckiest person on the face of the earth! ...*because of the love of God.*

Growing Panes

No. 6-21

Tribulations and Trials
Revelation 8:6 — Revelation 11:19

	INSIDE TRACK	MIDDLE LANES	FAST TRACK
Monday: Six Trumpets Sound	☐ Revelation 9:4	☐ Revelation 8:6-9:20 ☐ Numbers 10:1-6 ☐ Ezekiel 33:1-9	☐ Jeremiah 4:14-21 ☐ Exodus 9:18-26 ☐ Zechariah 9:1-11 ☐ Matthew 24:29-31 ☐ Luke 12:49-56
Tuesday: The Little Book	☐ Revelation 10:10	☐ Revelation 10:1-11 ☐ Genesis 9:12-17 ☐ Job 26:1-14; 37:5	☐ Psalm 29:1-11 ☐ Ezekiel 2:1-3:7 ☐ Daniel 12:1-9 ☐ Matthew 28:16-20 ☐ Hebrews 6:1-8
Wednesday: The Two Witnesses	☐ Revelation 11:12,13	☐ Revelation 11:1-14 ☐ Zechariah 2:1-10 ☐ 2 Kings 1:1-18	☐ Psalm 79:1-13 ☐ Hebrews 10:19-39 ☐ Luke 21:10-26 ☐ 1 Timothy 4:1-15 ☐
Thursday: The Seventh Trumpet Sounds	☐ Revelation 11:17,18	☐ Revelation 11:15-19 ☐ Matthew 19:23-28 ☐ Isaiah 9:1-7	☐ Exodus 15:12-17 ☐ Psalm 96:1-13 ☐ Hebrews 12:18-29 ☐ Luke 1:39-56 ☐
Friday: Faith Lessons for Today	☐ Psalm 103:13	☐ 1Thessalonians 4:13-5:11 ☐ Psalm 103:1-22 ☐ 1 Peter 5:6-11	☐ 2 Thessalonians 1:3-12 ☐ Hebrews 2:1-17 ☐ Colossians 2:6-15 ☐ 2 Thessalonians 2:1-17 ☐

Preacher's Stories -No.22

I am told that there is a particular species of eagle which builds its nest high up on the face of a cliff overlooking the sea. In this nest the eagle chick is hatched and spends its first days watching its mother come and go, collecting food and bringing it back.

One day mum decides it's time her chicks learned to fly. You know how she does it? She forces her way right into the nest and then pushes her chicks out. The chick starts plummeting down the cliff-face, terrified, shocked, heartbeat racing, aware that death is just seconds away. And then something amazing happens. The chick instinctively stretches the wings it never knew it had, the plummet becomes a fall, then a gentle rise. Soon the chick is soaring like its mother.

It's in that split second of terrifying danger that the chick comes face to face with itself, and face to face with wider reality.

In that terrifying moment the chick discovers what it is. And without that terrifying moment it will never learn to soar like an eagle.

Growing Panes
No. 6-22

	INSIDE TRACK	MIDDLE LANES	FAST TRACK
Monday: The Woman & Child	☐ Revelation 12:5	☐ Revelation 12:1-6 ☐ Luke 21:8-28 ☐ Acts 2:17-28	☐ Isaiah 27:1 ☐ Isaiah 66:7-12 ☐ Psalm 74:12-17 ☐ Hosea 2:14-20 ☐ Ezekiel 29:1-6
Tuesday: The War in Heaven	☐ Revelation 12:9	☐ Revelation 12:7-12 ☐ Daniel 12:5-13 ☐ Daniel 10:7-21	☐ Psalm 2:7-12 ☐ Psalm 96:1-13 ☐ Ephesians 3:10-12 ☐ Ephesians 6:10-17 ☐ 2 Peter 3:10-13
Wednesday: The War on Earth	☐ Revelation 12:17	☐ Revelation 12:13-17 ☐ 2 Corinthians 10:3-6 ☐ Jude 1:3-16	☐ Job 1:6-12 ☐ Job 2:1-7 ☐ Genesis 3:1-7 ☐ Matthew 4:1-10 ☐ Luke 12:49-51
Thursday: The Beasts	☐ Revelation 13:8	☐ Revelation 13:1-18 ☐ Daniel 2:31-44 ☐ Isaiah 17:12-13	☐ Daniel 7:15-25 ☐ Daniel 8:23-24 ☐ Psalm 2:1-6 ☐ 2 Thessalonians 2:3-4 ☐ 2 Corinthians 11:12-15
Friday: Faith Lessons for Today	☐ 1 Thessalonians 5:2	☐ 1 Thessalonians 5:1-11 ☐ Mark 10:29-31 ☐ Matthew 24:4-27	☐ 2 Timothy 3:1-17 ☐ 1 Peter 2:9-10 ☐ 1 Peter 5:8-11 ☐ Colossians 1:15-20 ☐

Preacher's Stories -No.23

Each week at the meetings of a local Rotary club a different member was asked to give a brief statement about his job. When it was the turn of a Christian minister, he stood up and said:

"I'm with a global enterprise. We have branches in every country in the world. We have our representatives in nearly every parliament and board room on earth. We're into motivation and behavior alteration.

"We are into life insurance and fire insurance. We perform spiritual heart transplants. Our original Organiz-

er owns all the real estate on earth plus an assortment of galaxies and constellations. He knows everything and lives everywhere. Our product is free for the asking. (There's not enough money to buy it.)

"Our CEO was born in a hick town, worked as a carpenter, didn't own a home, was misunderstood by his family, hated by enemies, walked on water, was condemned to death without a trial, and arose from the dead—I talk with him every day."

Growing Panes

No. 6-23

Judgment on the Earth

Revelation 14:1– Revelation 18:19

	INSIDE TRACK	MIDDLE LANES	FAST TRACK
Monday: The Saved Standing with the Lamb	☐ Revelation 14:7	☐ Revelation 14:1-20 ☐ Psalm 132:13-16 ☐ 1 Thessalonians 4:13-18	☐ Matthew 24:26-31 ☐ Matthew 25:31-46 ☐ Daniel 7:1-14 ☐ Hebrews 12:22-24 ☐
Tuesday: The Bowls of Judgment	☐ Revelation 16:15	☐ Revelation 15:1-16:21 ☐ Matthew 13:36-43 ☐ 2 Thessalonians 1:5-10	☐ Leviticus 26:14-26 ☐ Daniel 4:1-3 ☐ Daniel 12:1-4 ☐ 2 Thessalonians 2:1-12 ☐
Wednesday: The Great Harlot	☐ Revelation 17:1	☐ Revelation 17:1-18 ☐ Nahum 3:1-5 ☐ Isaiah 23:15-18	☐ Ezekiel 23:28-31 ☐ Genesis 11:1-9 ☐ Jeremiah 2:20-28 ☐ Micah 1:3-7 ☐
Thursday: Babylon the Great Destroyed	☐ Revelation 18:4	☐ Revelation 18:1-19 ☐ Isaiah 13:1-11 ☐ Isaiah 13:12-22	☐ Ezekiel 43:1-5 ☐ Jeremiah 51:6-10 ☐ Luke 17:22-25 ☐ Daniel 5:5-6 ☐ Daniel 5:22-28
Friday: Faith Lessons for Today	☐ Matthew 28:18	☐ Matthew 13:44-50 ☐ Ecclesiastes 12:13-14 ☐ Luke 21:29-36	☐ Acts 17:24-31 ☐ Galatians 4:28-31 ☐ Matthew 24:42-44 ☐ 1 Corinthians 15:20-28 ☐ Isaiah 24:4-6

Preacher's Stories -No.24

While playing basketball with some friends, Bernard Travaielle noticed a friendly old janitor who stayed late to lock up the gym when they left. He was reading his Bible while he waited. In fact, he noticed that the janitor was reading the Book of Revelation.

Bernard was surprised. Not just that the old man was reading his Bible, but that he was reading the Book of Revelation which is a very difficult book to understand.

"Do you understand what you are reading?" Bernard asked.

"Oh yes, I understand it" the janitor replied.

Now Bernard was really intrigued. Here was the book that baffled the scholars, that was the focus of every conspiracy theory known to man, and this old man, a janitor with limited formal education, claimed to understand it!

"You understand the Book of Revelation?! What do you think it means?" asked Bernard.

The old man looked up at him and very quietly said, *"It means that Jesus is gonna win."*

Growing Panes

No. 6-24

Heaven Rejoices
Revelation 18:20 – Revelation 19:21

	INSIDE TRACK	MIDDLE LANES	FAST TRACK
Monday: Heaven Rejoices in Victory	☐ Revelation 18:20	☐ Revelation 18:20-24 ☐ Jeremiah 51:48-50 ☐ Isaiah 44:21-23	☐ Psalm 69:34-36 ☐ Psalm 98:7-9 ☐ Psalm 148:1-6 ☐ Psalm 96:11-13 ☐ Isaiah 49:13
Tuesday: Worship to God in the Highest	☐ Revelation 19:2	☐ Revelation 19:1-8 ☐ Psalm 115:14-18 ☐ Psalm 134:1-3	☐ 2 Chronicles 29:8-11 ☐ Psalm 95:6-11 ☐ Zephaniah 3:9-13 ☐ Hebrews 9:13-15 ☐ 1 Peter 3:13-17
Wednesday: Marriage Feast of the Lamb	☐ Revelation 19:7	☐ Revelation 19:9-10 ☐ Luke 14:15-24 ☐ Isaiah 53:7-9	☐ Acts 8:32-33 ☐ Hebrews 9:23-28 ☐ Ephesians 5:25-33 ☐ 1 Peter 2:4-6 ☐
Thursday: Second Coming of Christ	☐ Revelation 19:13,14	☐ Revelation 19:11-21 ☐ 1 Thessalonians 4:16-18 ☐	☐ Luke 21:29-36 ☐ Matthew 24:42-44 ☐ Titus 2:11-14 ☐ Matthew 16:24-28 ☐ James 5:7-9
Friday: Faith Lessons for Today	☐ Hebrews 11:6	☐ Ephesians 2:4-10 ☐ Isaiah 12:2-6 ☐ Romans 1:16-17	☐ Hebrews 11:1-2 ☐ Matthew 17:20-21 ☐ Matthew 21:21-22 ☐ Luke 7:1-10 ☐ Mark 11:22-26

Preacher's Stories –No.25

An unknown author once said, "As a boy, I thought of heaven as a city with domes, spires, and beautiful streets, inhabited by angels.

By and by my little brother died, and I thought of heaven much as before, but with one inhabitant that I knew.

Then another died, and then some of my acquaintances, so in time I began to think of heaven as containing several people that I knew.

But it was not until one of my own little children died that I began to think I had treasure in heaven myself. Afterward another went, and yet another.

By that time I had so many acquaintances and children in heaven that I no more thought of it as a city merely with streets of gold but as a place full of inhabitants.

Now there are so many loved ones there *I sometimes think I know more people in heaven than I do on earth.*

Growing Panes

No. 6-25

The Final Victory
Revelation 20:1 — Revelation 21:8

DATES
_____ TO _____

	INSIDE TRACK	MIDDLE LANES	FAST TRACK
Monday: Satan is Bound	☐ Revelation 20:2,3	☐ Revelation 20:1-6 ☐ Genesis 3:8-15 ☐ 2 Peter 2:4-10	☐ Isaiah 14:12-15 ☐ Ezekiel 28:11-19 ☐ Matthew 13:36-43 ☐ Luke 11:14-20 ☐ Jude 1:5-7
Tuesday: The Deceiver Released	☐ Revelation 21:10	☐ Revelation 20:7-10 ☐ Genesis 3:1-7 ☐ 2 Thessalonians 2:5-12	☐ Daniel 8:19-25 ☐ Matthew 24:15-25 ☐ 2 Corinthians 4:1-6 ☐ 2 Corinthians 11:13-15 ☐ 2 Timothy 3:10-17
Wednesday: The Great White Throne	☐ Revelation 20:12	☐ Revelation 20:11-15 ☐ Isaiah 65:1-7 ☐ Matthew 25:31-46	☐ Psalm 110:1-7 ☐ Ecclesiastes 12:13-14 ☐ Jeremiah 25:30-31 ☐ Zephaniah 1:14-18 ☐ Matthew 22:1-14
Thursday: New Jerusalem Descends	☐ Revelation 21:8	☐ Revelation 21:1-8 ☐ Hebrews 11:8-16 ☐ Isaiah 65:17-25	☐ Galatians 4:26-31 ☐ Hebrews 12:18-29 ☐ Hebrews 13:9-14 ☐ 2 Peter 3:10-13 ☐
Friday: Faith Lessons for Today	☐ Isaiah 42:1-4	☐ Isaiah 11:1-9 ☐ I Corinthians 15:50-58 ☐	☐ Psalm 46:1-11 ☐ Isaiah 62:1-5 ☐ 1 Corinthians 15:20-28 ☐ 1 Corinthians 15:35-44 ☐

Preacher's Stories –No.26

○n a foggy evening of June 18, 1815 a man stood in the tower of England's Winchester Cathedral looking for a ship sending a signal by use of lights. All of England held its breath, wanting to know the outcome of the war between their military leader, the Duke of Wellington, and the French dictator Napoleon Bonaparte at the decisive Battle of Waterloo.

So, as he stood in the tower of Winchester Cathedral our man waited to relay the news that would determine England's future. The signal came just as a heavy fog was rolling in. He could only see the words: *"Wellington defeated."*

The man signaled to other stations and the news spread everywhere, bringing great gloom and sadness.

But then the fog lifted, and the message was sent again, this time in full: *"Wellington defeated ...the enemy"*.

Growing Panes
No. 6-26

There is nothing to be afraid of...

Solmon Rosenberg tells this story from his time in a Nazi concentration camp during World War II:

He, his wife, his two sons, and his mother were all arrested and relocated to a labor camp. The rules were simple: As long as you can do your work, you are permitted to live. When you become too weak to do your work, then you will be exterminated. The conditions were harsh and inhumane. The prisoners were given little to eat and the weak among them would begin to waste away until the inevitable day they could no longer work and they were taken to the gas chambers.

Rosenberg watched his mother and father being marched off to their deaths when they became too weak. He knew that his youngest son, David, would be next because David had always been a frail child.

Every evening when Rosenberg came back into the barracks after his hours of labor, he would search for the faces of his family. When he found them, they would huddle together, embrace one another, and thank God for another day of life. But each day, David looked just a little bit more frail, and Solomon always feared the next day would be the day he was taken away.

One day Rosenberg came back and couldn't find his family. He stormed through the barracks in a panic until he finally discovered his oldest son, Joshua, in a corner, huddled, weeping. He said, "Josh, tell me it's not true." Joshua turned and said, "It is true, Poppa. Today David was not strong enough to do his work, so they came for him."

"But where is your mother?" asked Mr. Rosenberg, "She is still strong enough to work!"

"Oh Poppa," he exclaimed. "When they came for David, he was afraid and he was crying.

Momma said, 'There is nothing to be afraid of, David,' and she pulled him close and held him. Then she took his hand and went with him so he wouldn't have to be alone."

-Author Unknown

		INSIDE TRACK	MIDDLE LANES	FAST TRACK
Monday: The City of God in Heaven		☐ Revelation 21:10	☐ Revelation 21:9-27 ☐ 2 Corinthians 12:2-4 ☐ Isaiah 2:1-3	☐ Isaiah 14:12-14 ☐ John 3:13-17 ☐ Matthew 7:20-22 ☐ Hebrews 11:8-16 ☐
Tuesday: No Night There		☐ Revelation 22:5	☐ Revelation 22:1-5 ☐ John 9:3-5 ☐ John 11:9-11	☐ Psalm 27:1-3 ☐ John 8:11-13 ☐ 1 John 2:1-15 ☐ Ephesians 5:8-14 ☐ 1 John 1:5-7
Wednesday: Victorious and Rewarded		☐ Revelation 22:12	☐ Revelation 22:6-13 ☐ Matthew 16:26-28 ☐ Hebrews 12:1-3	☐ 1 Peter 1:3-5 ☐ 2 Timothy 4:7-9 ☐ 1 Corinthians 9:24-26 ☐ 1 John 5:1-5 ☐
Thursday: Rights to the Tree of Life		☐ Revelation 22:18,19	☐ Revelation 22:14-21 ☐ Genesis 2:8-9 ☐ John 6:35-40	☐ Revelation 2:1-7 ☐ Psalm 118:19-24 ☐ 1 Corinthians 1:18-31 ☐ ☐
Friday: Faith Lessons for Today		☐ John 3:16-17	☐ John 1:9-14 ☐ John 4:21-24 ☐ John 10:1-18	☐ John 11:21-27 ☐ John 13:31-35 ☐ John 14:1-4 ☐ John 17:20-26 ☐ John 21:15-25

Preacher's Stories -No.27

An old Indian father to test the prowess of his three sons, pointed to a mountain that was bold against the sky and said,

"Go climb that mountain!" ...Bring back proof of how high you climbed."

After several days one of them returned. He told of going through forests of the giant trees and seeing the beautiful green foliage of a thousand flowering plants.

He brought back a rare flower that only grows high up on the mountain. The father knew he had gotten to the timberline.

Later, the second son returned carrying a hard-red flint stone. He also told of seeing the beauty of God's nature on his climb. The second son had gotten high above the timberline where there was no longer any vegetation.

Many days later the third son returned and said,

"I come back empty-handed. Where I stood there was nothing but ice and snow. But, I stood on the peak and looked out over a vast valley where two rivers flowed together into a mighty sea."

The father knew he had reached the summit, and said:
"You brought back something greater than the others, you now have *a vision in your soul.*"

Growing Panes
No. 6-27

Race Review Quiz

One question is taken from each of the 27 weeks of the race. This is an open book test, go to the week number (Question #) to check your answers.

1) *When the Word became flesh we saw*
   A) The power of God
   B) The glory of God
   C) The justice of God

2) *To enter the Kingdom of God, one must*
   A) Stop living in the world
   B) Be virtuous and worthy
   C) Be reborn

3) *How many times had the Samaritan woman been married?*
   A) Once
   B) Five times
   C) Four times

4) *The man healed at the pool of Bethesda had been paralyzed for*
   A) 36 years
   B) 37 years
   C) 38 years

5) *Jesus walked on the water at*
   A) The Sea of Capernaum
   B) The Sea of Galilee
   C) The Sea of Tiberias

6) *According to the prophets, the Messiah was to come from*
   A) Bethlehem
   B) Galilee
   C) Nazareth

7) *The blind man could see after washing his eyes in*
   A) The pool of Siloam
   B) The Bethesda pool
   C) The Jordan river

8) *Lazarus was raised from the dead in the city of*
   A) Nazareth
   B) Bethany
   C) Jerusalem

9) *John quotes this prophet to show the glory of Christ*
   A) Jeremiah
   B) Obadiah
   C) Isaiah

10) *This disciple did not want Jesus to wash his feet:*
    A) Judas
    B) James
    C) Peter

11) *The main lesson for us in the vine and the branches is*
    A) To bear fruit
    B) To stay connected with Christ
    C). To love one another

12) *Mostly, Jesus addressed his prayers to:*
    A) Almighty God
    B) Father
    C) Friend

13) *Jesus was first taken before this man after his arrest*
    A) Caiaphas
    B) Pilate
    C) Annas

14) *This man sentenced Jesus to die*
    A) Caiaphas
    B) Herod
    C) Pilate

15) *Which of these disciples outran the other to the tomb:*
    A) Peter outran John
    B) John outran Peter
    C) Timothy outran them both

16) *Three times Jesus asked Peter:*
    A) Will you obey me?
    B) Have you confessed me?
    C) Do you love me?

17) *John used love between brothers to illustrate brotherly love*
    A) Cain and Abel
    B) Joseph and his brothers
    C) James and John

18) *The Book of Revelation was first addressed to*
    A) Seven churches in Asia
    B) The church in Rome
    C) The church in Jerusalem

19) *This church was told to be faithful to the point of death*
    A) Ephesus
    B) Smyrna
    C) Thyatira

20) *This church was lukewarm*
    A) Laodicea
    B) Philadelphia
    C) Antioch

21) *John saw death riding on the pale horse under the fourth seal*
    A) True
    B) False

22) *When John opened the seventh seal, on earth there was*
    A) Bolts of lightening and fire
    B) Silence for thirty minutes
    C) 144,000 standing with God

23) *In heaven, this angel fought against the Devil and his angels, and they were cast out.*
    A) Gabriel
    B) Lucifer
    C) Michael

24) *John heard a voice from heaven say, Write this down, Blessed are those who...*
    A) Keep their robes white
    B) Sing the new song
    C) Die in the Lord

25) *John saw a white horse with a rider dressed in dazzling white, with this written on his robe and on his thigh:*
    A) King of Kings and Lord of Lords
    B) Faithful and True
    C) The Word of God

26) *John saw the books were opened and everyone was judged. Those thrown into the lake of fire were:*
    A) Names not in Book of Life
    B) The red dragon
    C) The beast from the abyss

27) *In the new city of Jerusalem, there will be no temple, no sun, no closed gates*
    A) True
    B) False

www.ingramcontent.com/pod-product-compliance
Lightning Source LLC
Chambersburg PA
CBHW041221040426
42443CB00002B/35